Savor
DETROIT

Let your taste buds *Savor* more than 140 recipes
from the city's most celebrated chefs.

PRESENTED BY

HOUR
DETROIT

Published by Momentum Books, L.L.C.
117 West Third Street
Royal Oak, MI 48067

ISBN: 978-1-938018-08-4
LCCN: 2015933165

On the Front Cover:
Cabernet Braised Beef Short Rib | Chef Meyer

On the Back Cover:
Skeleton Key

Chef and Food Photography by: *Martin Vecchio*
Event Photography by: *EE Berger*
Text by: *Casey Nesterowich*
Design by: *Katie M. Sachs*

INTRODUCTION

It's been said that one of the fastest, if not *the* fastest, way to a person's heart is through the stomach. And in the past few years, it's safe to say metro Detroit has been winning over even the pickiest eaters.

If you live here or grew up here, you've always known the city has been full of options beyond the coney dog. But recently, we've drawn curiosity from food fans around the globe.

Nearly every week brings news of another eatery — in downtown, Midtown, and beyond, abandoned buildings are being refurbished and shaped into restaurants. Suburban mainstays are getting multimillion-dollar face-lifts. And a new batch of chefs and investors are lining up to join the party.

Consider some recent new "finer dining" options like Wright & Co., Bistro 82, Selden Standard, Antietam, and Top of the Pontch. Then think of the wonderful standbys and semi-recent newcomers: Forest Grill, The Root Restaurant & Bar, Marais, The Lark, The Silver Spoon, Cuisine, Hong Hua, Coach Insignia, Roast, Torino, Bacco, Tre Monti, The Whitney, Joe Muer Seafood, Iridescence… the list goes on.

There seem to be so many more to come — not to mention a growing throng of pop-ups — that the phrase "most anticipated opening" is starting to become as overused as "foodie."

The city itself has a heartbeat again, and it's louder than ever before. So it seems like the perfect time to present *Hour Detroit's* first cookbook. Why now? Instead, you might ask, "What took you so long?"

In 1996, the first issue of *Hour Detroit* was printed, and it quickly became the source Detroiters could rely on for award-winning coverage of issues and people affecting their lives. The culinary scene has been a significant part of the mix. We've reviewed every type of cuisine and showcased metro Detroit's best spots, including the coveted "Restaurant of the Year." And many of the chefs contributing recipes to this book have hung their aprons at some of these extraordinary establishments.

If you've attended one of our Savor Detroit events, you know you're in for a treat. If you haven't been to one (or more) of our five-night dinner series, you'll love what's in store. Inside these pages are recipes from the 2014 Savor Detroit dinners. There are also wine pairings for each dish and cocktail recipes from the talented folks at The Sugar House. We profile the chefs behind these amazing dishes as well as the artists who brought their work to our dinner events to benefit local charities.

This project has truly been a labor of love for all of us who got to be a part of it, and represents much of what we stand for here at *Hour Detroit* magazine. We hope you hold on to this cookbook for a long time, as a testament to Detroit's growing reputation in the culinary world. And stay tuned; this will be just the first in a series of annual cookbooks for you to "Savor" along with us.

Contents

30   60   126

The Menus · Spring

MONDAY

Appetizer
GOUGÈRE
Tapenade, whipped goat cheese | *Prepared by Chef Rigato*
Wine: *Mountain Cuvee, Gundlach Bundschu, Sonoma, Calif. (2011),*
Pinot Grigio, Cantine Riondo, Veneto, Italy (2013)

Appetizer
HOUSE GRAVLAX
Pumpernickel crostini, horseradish, pickle | *Prepared by Chef Gilbert*
Wine: *Mountain Cuvee, Gundlach Bundschu, Sonoma, Calif. (2011),*
Pinot Grigio, Cantine Riondo, Veneto, Italy (2013)

Appetizer
FRESH RICOTTA AGNOLOTTI SPOONS
Tomato marmalade, lemon reduction | *Prepared by Chef Gilbert*
Wine: *Mountain Cuvee, Gundlach Bundschu, Sonoma, Calif. (2011),*
Pinot Grigio, Cantine Riondo, Veneto, Italy (2013)

One
GRILLED BABY OCTOPUS
Warm Sunseed Farms potato salad, favas, olives, romesco | *Prepared by Chef Rigato*
Wine: *Do Ferreiro Albarino (2012), Rias Baixas, Spain*

Two
SCALLOP
Smoked potato mousse, beet couscous, & shellfish emulsion | *Prepared by Chef Rigato*
Wine: *Domaine Vacheron Sancerre Blanc, Loire, France (2011)*

Three
LOCAL RABBIT CONFIT
Ricotta gnocchi, spring pea, garlic, ramps, morels, rabbit broth | *Prepared by Chef Rigato*
Wine: *Costa di Bussia Barolo, Piemonte, Italy (2009)*

Four
PISTACHIO-CRUSTED LAMB
Merguez, carrot purée, candied grapefruit peel | *Prepared by Chef Gilbert*
Wine: *Ernesto Cantena Cabernet Sauvignon Siesta, Mendoza, Argentina (2010)*

Dessert
PASTRY COLLABORATION
Prepared by Chef Rigato and Chef Gilbert
Wine/Coffee: *Chateau d'Orignac Pineau des Charente, Cognac, France.*
Kona Blend courtesy of Cadillac Coffee Co.

TUESDAY

Appetizer
SUSHI MAKIMONO ROLLS
Prepared by Chef Ward
Wine: *NV Andreola Dirupo Prosecco DOCG, Valdobbiadene (2008),*
Domaine de Triennes "St. Auguste," Provence

Appetizer
VITELLO TONNE
Seared veal tenderloin, ahi tuna sashimi, anchovy caper sauce | *Prepared by Chef Casadei*
Wine: *NV Andreola Dirupo Prosecco DOCG, Valdobbiadene (2008),*
Domaine de Triennes "St. Auguste," Provence

One
ALASKAN HALIBUT
Over an Alaskan king crabcake served with asparagus tips &
hon shimeji mushrooms, with an orange beurre blanc | *Prepared by Chef Ward*
Wine: *Chateau de Maligny (2010), Chablis 1er Cru "Fourchaume"*

Two
PACCHERI CON VELUTATA DI POMODORO PASTA
With fresh ricotta, Parmigiano-Reggiano, spinach, tomato purée, chives
Prepared by Chef Casadei
Wine: *Tenuta Trecciano (2011), Chianti Colli Senesi*

Three
CORIANDER-CRUSTED 'BIG EYE' TUNA
Served with haricot verts, fingerling potatoes, nicoise olives, chimichurri | *Prepared by Chef Ward*
Wine: *Domaine La Barroche "Signature" Chateauneuf du Pape (2010)*

Four
DRY-AGED COLORADO RACK OF LAMB
Truffle polenta, rapini salsa verde, port wine balsamic reduction | *Prepared by Chef Casadei*
Wine: *Collazzi "Super Tuscan" IGT, Toscana (2010)*

Dessert
COCONUT SNOWBALL
Served with crushed pineapple beignet with basil gelato, pear compote
Prepared by Chef Casadei
Wine/Coffee: *La Fleur Renaissance Sautérnes, Bordeaux (2011)*
Guatemala Huehuetenango courtesy of Cadillac Coffee Co.

WEDNESDAY

Appetizer
TARTARE DE THON SUR LES GATEAUX DE RISOTTO
Tuna tartare on risotto cakes | *Prepared by Chef Grosz*
Wine: *Due Torri Pinot Grigio, Due Torri Pinot Noir*

Appetizer
RENFORCER A COURT DE LOIS ANGLAIS
Beef short rib on English peas | *Prepared by Chef Grosz*
Wine: *Due Torri Pinot Grigio, Due Torri Pinot Noir*

Appetizer
MIALE TONATO
Roast pork, tuna anchovy sauce, fried caper, roasted pepper | *Prepared by Chef Del Signore*
Wine: *Due Torri Pinot Grigio, Due Torri Pinot Noir*

Appetizer
CAPONATA
Sicilian vegetable stew, cucumber cup | *Prepared by Chef Del Signore*
Wine: *Due Torri Pinot Grigio, Due Torri Pinot Noir*

One
COLD DUCK THREE WAYS
Torchon with strawberry jelly, duck ham, duck terrine | *Prepared by Chef Grosz*
Wine: *Chateau St. Didier-Parnac Canors Malbec*

Two
TORTELLINI BRODO DI CAPPONE
Capon-stuffed pasta, capon broth, celery leaves, roasted trumpet mushrooms
Prepared by Chef Del Signore
Wine: *Cesari Boscarel*

Three
ROASTED STURGEON
With crawfish, fennel, orange | *Prepared by Chef Grosz*
Wine: *Domaine Roux Bourgogne Chardonnay*

Four
GUANCIA DI VITELLO ARROSTO
Braised veal cheek, polenta, cipollini, Brussels sprouts | *Prepared by Chef Del Signore*
Wine: *Cesari Jema*

Dessert
MOUSSE AL CIOCCOLATO
Valrhona dark chocolate, chocolate espresso, tuile, caramel, cashews, vanilla gelato | *Prepared by Chef Del Signore*
Wine/Coffee: *Cesari Mara European French Roast courtesy of Cadillac Coffee Co.*

THURSDAY

Appetizer
GOLDEN DEEP-FRIED BABY GARLIC RIBS
With peanut sauce | *Prepared by Chef Chan*
Wine: Alta Vista Malbec, Mendoza NV Punkt Genau, Austria

Appetizer
CURRIED CHICKEN SATAY
With hoisin sauce glaze | *Prepared by Chef Somerville*
Wine: Alta Vista Malbec, Mendoza NV Punkt Genau, Austria

One
JADE & PEARL
Chinese muga with scallop and X.O. sauce | *Prepared by Chef Chan*
Wine: Black Star Farms Arcturos Dry Riesling, Old Mission Peninsula (2011)

Two
CRISP ROAST DUCK
With Comtè cheese dumplings, wilted garlic spinach, blood orange sauce
Prepared by Chef Somerville
Wine: Elio Perrone "Tasmorcan" Barbera d'Asti, Piemonte (2012)

Three
SAUTÉED SKATE
With spring corn risotto & Meyer lemon emulsion | *Prepared by Chef Somerville*
Wine: Becker Estate Pinot Blanc, Rheinphalz (2010)

Four
BRAISED SHORT RIB
With onions & black pepper sauce | *Prepared by Chef Chan*
Wine: Buil & Gine "Gine Gine" Priorat, Cataluna (2011)

Dessert
ROASTED WHITE CHOCOLATE AND BLACKBERRY GATEAU
With five-spice poached pineapple & coconut tuile | *Prepared by Chef Somerville*
Wine/Coffee: NV '42' Vidal Ice Wine, Lake Michigan Shore,
Colombian Supremo courtesy of Cadillac Coffee Co.

FRIDAY

Appetizer
DUCK RILLETTE
Smoked blue cheese, braised fig chutney on crostini | *Prepared by Chef Green*
Wine: *Domaine de Millet, Cotes Blanc de Gascogne (2012),*
Georges Vigouroux "Pigmentum" Malbec, Cahors (2011)

Appetizer
SMOKED SALMON
Prepared by Chef Hollyday
Wine: *Domaine de Millet, Cotes Blanc de Gascogne (2012),*
Georges Vigouroux "Pigmentum" Malbec, Cahors (2012)

One
ESCABECHE OF MICHIGAN SHRIMP
Tomato fennel, relish, parsley coulis, fingerling gaufrette | *Prepared by Chef Green*
Wine: *Henri de Richemer "Terre & Mer" Terret Gris, Cotes de Thau (2011)*

Two
SWEET PEA AGNOLOTTI
Burrata, mushroom, asparagus | *Prepared by Chef Hollyday*
Wine: *Chateau de Fontenille Blanc, Bordeaux (2012)*

Three
GRILLED TROUT PEPERONATA
Arugula salad, black olive jus | *Prepared by Chef Green*
Wine: *Domaine de Roche Guillon, Beaujolais-Villages (2011)*

Four
ROAST LAMB
Preserved lemon, artichoke | *Prepared by Chef Hollyday*
Wine: *Domaine des Pasquiers, Cotes du Rhone (2011)*

Dessert
FROZEN AMARETTO SABAYON
Citrus mint salad, pine nut granola | *Prepared by Chef Green*
Wine/Coffee: *Chateau Belingard, Monbazillac (2009)*
Sumatra Kuda Mas courtesy of Cadillac Coffee Co.

SPRING COCKTAILS | MONDAY THROUGH FRIDAY:
Vodka Basil Smash | PAMA Spritz | Bourbon Manhattan | Skeleton Key
Vodka Caipirinha | PAMA Daisy | Texas 75 | PAMA Swizzle | Molecular Mule

MONDAY

Appetizer

ATLANTIC SALMON MOUSSE

In a cucumber wheel | *Prepared by Chef Dell'Acqua*

Wine: *Zardetto, Zeta Prosecco Superiore, Veneto, Italy (2012), Marques de Grinon,*
Caliza (Syrah / Petit Verdot), Dominio de Valdepusa, Spain (2009)

Appetizer

COUNTRY HAM PÂTÉ MARIGOLDS

Pickled green strawberries | *Prepared by Chef Lipar*

Wine: *Zardetto, Zeta Prosecco Superiore, Veneto, Italy (2012),*
Marques de Grinon, Caliza (Syrah / Petit Verdot), Dominio de Valdepusa, Spain (2009)

One

HARVEST VEGETABLES

Carrots, beets, Brussels sprouts | *Prepared by Chef Lipar*

Wine: *Ceretto, Arneis Biange, Piedmont, Italy (2013)*

Two

TORTELLACCIO

Big tortellino stuffed with braised beef served with a cream of porcini mushroom & leeks
Prepared by Chef Dell'Acqua

Wine: *Castello di Neive, Barbaresco, Piedmont, Italy (2009)*

Three

WALLEYE

Walleye, preserved lemon, Swiss chard | *Prepared by Chef Lipar*

Wine: *Mastroberardino, Falanghini di Sannio, Campania, Italy (2012)*

Four

FILETTINO DI VITELLO

Veal medallion, Gorgonzola cheese, served on grilled polenta & balsamic vinaigrette sauce
Prepared by Chef Dell'Acqua

Wine: *Valdipiatta, Vino Novile di Montepulciano, Tuscany, Italy (2010)*

Dessert

BLACKBERRY BREAD PUDDING

Fermented blackberries, bread pudding, buttermilk | *Prepared by Chef Lipar*

Wine: *Campbells, Rutherglen Topaque, Australia*

TUESDAY

Appetizer
DUCK FAT POPCORN
With gin salt | *Prepared by Chef Meyer*
Wine: *Domaine de Nizas Rosé, Coteaux de Languedoc, France (2013),*
Loimer Grüner Veltliner, Kamptal, Austria (2012)

Appetizer
'CHICKEN CHICKEN'
Cracklin, liver, compressed apple | *Prepared by Chef Rigato*
Wine: *Domaine de Nizas Rosé, Coteaux de Languedoc, France (2013),*
Loimer Grüner Veltliner, Kamptal, Austria (2012)

Appetizer
BLISS SMOKED STEELHEAD ROE
Cantaloupe gelee, crème fraiche, celery, cucumber, black pepper | *Prepared by Chef Meyer*
Wine: *Domaine de Nizas Rosé, Coteaux de Languedoc, France (2013),*
Loimer Grüner Veltliner, Kamptal, Austria (2012)

One
MICHIGAN LAMB CRUDO
Red onion, house preserved lemon, yogurt, curried squash, naan | *Prepared by Chef Rigato*
Wine: *Trimbach Reserve Pinot Gris, Alsace, France (2011)*

Two
WHAT THE DUCK *#%!
Maple-glazed duck breast tasso, apple-scented duck mousse, duck confit spring roll,
pumpernickel toast, frisee, orange-apple gastrique | *Prepared by Chef Meyer*
Wine: *Famille Perrin Vinsobres "Les Cornuds" AOC Vinsobres, Rhone Valley, France (2011)*

Three
HOISIN & CAB-BRAISED BEEF SHORT RIB
Vanilla-ginger sweet potato, amaranth, edamame, walnut, bruleed bay scallop | *Prepared by Chef Meyer*
Wine: *Nine Stones Shiraz, Barossa, Australia (2011)*

Four
BLISS SMOKED STEELHEAD ROE
Cantaloupe gelee, crème fraiche, celery, cucumber, black pepper | *Prepared by Chef Meyer*
Wine: *Domaine de Nizas Rosé, Coteaux de Languedoc, France (2013),*
Loimer Grüner Veltliner, Kamptal, Austria (2012)

Dessert
DARK CHOCOLATE VS. CHEESE
Tanzanie "Origine Rare" dark chocolate, coffee, butterscotch, amaro
Delice de Bourgogne:
Cinnamon-vanilla risotto cake, black walnut, fig compote, lemon powder
Prepared by Chef Rigato
Wine: *Warre's 10-year "Otima" Tawny Port, Portugal*

WEDNESDAY

Appetizer
'STEAK FRITES' GAUFRETTE
Piedmontese short rib, horseradish tarragon aioli | *Prepared by Chef Polisei*
Wine: *Biutiful Cava Brut Rosé, Spain Duck Pond Pinot Noir, Willamette Valley, Oregon (2012)*

Appetizer
MINIATURE LOBSTER ROLLS
Prepared by Chef Halberg
Wine: *Biutiful Cava Brut Rosé, Spain Duck Pond Pinot Noir, Willamette Valley, Oregon (2012)*

One
CHARRED OCTOPUS
Pickled watermelon, green tomato gazpacho | *Prepared by Chef Halberg*
Wine: *Chateau Bouscasse Blanc, Madiran, France (2010)*

Two
PORK BELLY CONFIT
Oyster beignet, sweet corn purée, apple chow-chow | *Prepared by Chef Polisei*
Wine: *Roux Pere et Fils Chardonnay "Les Murelles," Burgundy, France (2013)*

Three
BLACK COD
Fall squash tortelloni, sage brown butter, winter truffle | *Prepared by Chef Polisei*
Wine: *Cantine San Silvestro "Brumo" Nebbiolo Alba, Piemonte, Italy (2011)*

Four
BREAST OF SQUAB
Fricassee of leg, roasted fig, cippoline, baby carrot | *Prepared by Chef Halberg*
Wine: *Costa di Bussia Arcapla, Piedmont, Italy (2009)*

Dessert
RED WINE POACHED PEACH
Whipped mascarpone, pistachio shortbread cookie | *Prepared by Chef Polisei*
Wine: *Ariola Lambrusco dell'Emilia "Marcello," Emilio-Romagna, Italy*

FALL COCKTAILS | MONDAY THROUGH FRIDAY:
Kentucky Mule | Tiger in the Jungle | Cucumber Spritz | El Conquistador
Sugar House Manhattan | St. Croix Daiquiri | Cucumber Crush | El Diablo

THURSDAY

Appetizer
TORCHON OF FOIE GRAS
On brioche with pickled Michigan leeks | *Prepared by Chef Polcyn*
Wine: *Tolol Sauvignon Blanc, Chile (2013), Tolol Cabernet Sauvignon, Chile (2011)*

Appetizer
SAVORY GOUGÈRES
Filled with Mornay sauce & local cheese | *Prepared by Chef Polcyn*
Wine: *Tolol Sauvignon Blanc, Chile (2013), Tolol Cabernet Sauvignon, Chile (2011)*

Appetizer
GRILLED CHORIZO
Blue Asiago, dried plums | *Prepared by Chef Johns*
Wine: *Tolol Sauvignon Blanc, Chile (2013), Tolol Cabernet Sauvignon, Chile (2011)*

Appetizer
ROASTED SQUASH AND MICHIGAN SHRIMP DUMPLINGS
With pickled chilies | *Prepared by Chef Johns*
Wine: *Tolol Sauvignon Blanc, Chile (2013), Tolol Cabernet Sauvignon, Chile (2011)*

One
MELO FARMS MULEFOOT PORCHETTA
Sauce gribiche, field arugula, lemon | *Prepared by Chef Polcyn*
Wine: *Cornerstone Cellars "Syrah Rose," Napa Valley, Calif. (2013)*

Two
FENNEL-HAKUREI TURNIP SALAD
Fall greens, honey-white vinaigrette | *Prepared by Chef Johns*
Wine: *Dr. Hermann Riesling "Slate Vineyard," Mosel, Germany (2012)*

Three
BRIOCHE-CRUSTED WALLEYE
Ragout of local mushrooms, blue potatoes, mustard greens | *Prepared by Chef Johns*
Wine: *Triennes Sainte Fleur "Viognier," Provence, France (2011)*

Four
PAN-ROASTED BREAST OF INDIANA DUCKLING
Ballotine of leg and thigh, roasted end-of-the season corn, charred heirloom tomatoes,
caramelized Imlay City shallot tart | *Prepared by Chef Polcyn*
Wine: *Core Elevation Sensation "Grenache/Mourvedre Blend," Santa Barbara County, Calif. (2008)*

Dessert
VARIATIONS OF CHOCOLATE & BEET
Raspberries, black pepper ice cream | *Prepared by Chef Johns*
Wine: *La Fleur Renaissance "Sautérnes," Bordeaux, France (2011)*

FRIDAY

Appetizer
CRISPY SMOKED PORK EPIGRAM
Butternut Squash & maple mustard BBQ sauce | Prepared by Chef Constantine
Wine: *Mionetto Prosecco, Italy, Oyster Bay Pinot Noir, Marlborough, New Zealand (2013)*

Appetizer
CROQUE MADAME
Topped with quail eggs | Prepared by Chef Constantine
Wine: *Mionetto Prosecco, Italy, Oyster Bay Pinot Noir, Marlborough, New Zealand (2013)*

Appetizer
RED GRAPE MACAROONS
With foie gras, cherry compote | Prepared by Chef Yagihashi
Wine: *Mionetto Prosecco, Italy, Oyster Bay Pinot Noir, Marlborough, New Zealand (2013)*

Appetizer
SPANISH POTATO OMELET
With mentaiko | Prepared by Chef Yagihashi
Wine: *Mionetto Prosecco, Italy, Oyster Bay Pinot Noir, Marlborough, New Zealand (2013)*

One
PISTACHIO-ENCRUSTED SAVORY GOAT CHEESE ICE CREAM SANDWICH
With green apple & arugula slaw | Prepared by Chef Constantine
Wine: *Domaine Vacheron Guigne Chevres (2011)*

Two
SEARED MAINE SCALLOPS
With soba gnocchi & celery root foam | Prepared by Chef Yagihashi
Wine: *Chateau de la Font Du Loup Chateauneuf Blanc (2012)*

Three
PAN-SEARED DUCK BREAST
Wilted kale, roasted chanterelles, quinoa cake, buttercup squash purée | Prepared by Chef Constantine
Wine: *Domaine Vacheron Belle Dame Rouge (2009)*

Four
GRILLED BEEF SHORT RIBS
Crispy veal sweetbreads & pickled tongue, Brussels sprout salad, aromatic sauce
Prepared by Chef Yagihashi
Wine: *Chateau de la Font Du Loup Chateauneuf Red (2013)*

Dessert
JAPANESE GREEN TEA SOUFFLE
Honey ginger crème anglaise, sesame cookie | Prepared by Chef Constantine
Wine: *Mio Sparkling Sake*

FEATURED ARTIST

Jenny Risher

Jenny Risher is a graduate of Detroit's The College For Creative Studies. Her continual strive for perfection, fresh style, and natural sensibility has afforded her the opportunity to photograph for many illustrious clients. Her photographs have been published in numerous national advertising and editorial publications.

Risher's car and dog series exhibit, created for Savor Detroit, was inspired by her sons Alex and Oliver's favorite book, P.D. Eastman's (Dr. Seuss'), *Go, Dog Go!*.

Risher completed her first book, *Heart Soul Detroit*, where she interviewed and photographed 50 iconic Detroiters, including Iggy Pop, Smokey Robinson, Jack White, Dr. Jack Kevorkian, Lily Tomlin, Eminem, and Tim Allen. A portion of the proceeds from her book signing at the event benefitted Gleaners Community Food Bank of Southeastern Michigan.

Tony Roko

Tony Roko is a Detroit native and self-taught artist whose dazzling images are created from re-purposed industrial and architectural materials. Roko's works are technically masterful and bold, filled with color that reaches out and grabs you, and faces that tell a story you cannot wait to hear. Guests at Savor Detroit had the unique opportunity to watch Roko bring an original piece of artwork to life as he painted a model at the event. Each night guests were able to browse a pop-up gallery of his work and bid on pieces during a silent auction, with a portion of the proceeds benefiting Forgotten Harvest.

Ten Nights, Twenty Chefs...

One Delicious Experience.

Each night, two local chefs and their team of employees pair up to prepare a five-course meal for 150 guests.

 During each Savor Detroit event, guests enjoy live music.

The Sugar House staff mixes
up a variety of cocktails
and aperitifs each night.

Appetizers are passed
during cocktail hour,
as the kitchen prepares
for dinner service.

Setting up 150 plates at once is no easy task,
and Great Lakes Culinary Center's open kitchen allows
every diner to view their dishes being prepared.

Bliss Smoked Steelhead Roe,
Recipe on page 54.

Appetizers

Crispy Smoked Pork Epigram

with Butternut Squash Slaw & Whole Grain Mustard Maple BBQ Sauce

CHEF CONSTANTINE | SERVES: 10

Ingredients:

2 pounds smoked pork butt, pulled and shredded

1 1/2 cups smoked ham hock stock

2 cups all-purpose flour

6 large eggs, whisked

2 cups panko breadcrumbs

Directions:

1| In a large bowl combine hot pulled pork and ham hock stock together. Adjust seasoning with salt and pepper. Place mixture on a cookie sheet lined with parchment paper. Make sure to spread out mixture evenly and chill until firm to the touch, about 3 hours or overnight.

2| Place flour, whisked eggs, and breadcrumbs in three separate bowls.

3| Remove pork from refrigerator, cut in small squares. First dip it in flour, then into the egg, and lastly into the bread-crumbs. Place on a cookie sheet and finish the remaining pork squares.

4| Heat the oil in a large skillet over medium-low heat, add 5-6 patties, cover, and cook for 3 minutes until the bottoms are deeply browned.

5| Flip the patties with a spatula and cook the second sides for 3 minutes, or until golden. Remove from the skillet and cool on a large plate while you cook the remaining patties. Add more oil to the skillet if needed between each batch.

Butternut Squash Slaw
Ingredients:

    1 1/2 tablespoons honey

    3 tablespoons extra-virgin olive oil

    2 teaspoons apple cider vinegar

    1/2 lemon, juiced

    Kosher salt and freshly ground black pepper

    1 medium butternut squash

    1 shallot, sliced thinly

    1 serrano pepper, sliced thinly

    2 tablespoons chopped parsley leaves

Directions:

1| In a large mixing bowl combine honey, olive oil, vinegar, and lemon juice. Season with salt and pepper. Stir well with a whisk until fully combined.

2| Remove the top narrow portion of the squash and peel. Discard or save the bulb portion for another use. Using a mandoline or sharp knife, cut the peeled cylinder into fine long matchsticks (julienne). This should yield about 4 cups. Fold into the dressing along with shallots, serrano pepper, and chopped fresh parsley.

Whole Grain Mustard Maple BBQ Sauce
Ingredients:

    1 tablespoon oil

    1/2 cup onion, diced

    2 cloves garlic, chopped

    5 tablespoons maple syrup

    2 cups ketchup

    3 tablespoon whole grain mustard

    4 tablespoons brown sugar

    3 tablespoons bourbon

    3 tablespoons apple cider vinegar

    1 teaspoon sea salt

    Dash of ground pepper

    1/2 teaspoon cayenne, or less to taste

Directions:

1| Place medium saucepan over medium heat. Heat oil in pan then add onions and sauté for 5 minutes. Add garlic and sauté for 2 minutes. Add the remaining ingredients and turn heat down to medium-low. Cook for 30 minutes stirring occasionally.

2| Remove from heat and allow to cool, then blend in blender and serve with pork.

Ham Hock Stock
Ingredients:

    5 smoked ham hocks

    1 carrot, chopped

    1 onion, quartered

    2 stalks celery

    5 thyme sprigs

    2 bay leaves

    1 teaspoon peppercorns

    4 quarts water

Directions:

1| Bring all of the ingredients to a boil in a large soup pot. Cover partially and simmer until the ham hock stock is flavorful and the meat is falling off the bones, about 2 hours.

2| Strain the stock and skim off any fat from the surface.

Torchon of Foie Gras

on Brioche with Pickled Leeks

CHEF POLCYN | SERVES: 5-6

Torchon de Foie Gras Seasoning Ratio

(Per 2 1/4 pounds foie gras)

> **2 teaspoons kosher salt**
>
> **1/2 teaspoon pepper** (white or very fine black)
>
> **1/2 teaspoon sugar**
>
> **1/2 teaspoon sodium nitrite** (pink salt)
>
> **2 teaspoons cognac or Sautérnes** (optional)
>
> **Milk, for soaking the foie gras**
>
> *You can purchase foie gras at a local grocery store or online.*

Directions:

Day 1:

1| Pull apart the lobes and remove as many veins from the foie gras as possible. Remove any sinew or membranes from the outside of the foie. If there are any bruised parts, cut them away and discard.

2| Working from the bottom of the lobes, butterfly them and locate the primary vein in the center of each. Slice through the lobe to the vein, following its path and pulling the foie apart to see the vein clearly. (Don't worry if you mangle the foie, better to get the veins out.)

3| Put the foie gras in a baking dish and cover with milk. Press plastic wrap down onto the surface of the liquid. Refrigerate overnight or for up to 2 days.

Day 2:

1| Drain and rinse the foie gras. Combine the salt, pepper, sugar, and pink salt. Sprinkle the seasoning all over the foie gras.

2| Press the foie into a container in an even layer 1 inch thick. Sprinkle it with the cognac or Sautérnes if using. Press a piece of plastic directly against the foie gras so as little air as possible is in contact with it. Refrigerate overnight.

Day 3:

1| Forming, cooking, and hanging the torchon: Remove the foie from the container and let it rest for an hour or so at room temperature (it will be easier to work with). Place it on a piece of parchment paper (best) or plastic wrap (will suffice) in the form of a loaf about 6 inches long and 3 inches wide. Roll the foie into a log, twisting and squeezing the ends of the parchment paper or plastic to help compact the foie.

2| Unwrap the foie, discard the paper or plastic and transfer the log to a piece of cheesecloth about 1 foot by 2 feet. Place the foie on the short end of the cheesecloth. Begin to roll it to force the foie into a compact log again.

3| Using butchers twine, loop a length of string around your index finger. With the same hand, hold one end of the cheesecloth tightly and wind the string around the end of the foie. Continue wrapping the string about 1/4 inch into the foie gras. This will help force the foie gras to compress into a tight roll, tie it off. Repeat the procedure on the other end. Tie a few ties along its girth for extra support.

4| In a wide pot, bring enough stock or water to submerge the foie gras to a simmer. Prepare an ice bath. Place the torchon into gently simmering liquid for 90 seconds. Immediately remove the torchon to the ice bath to cool for 5-10 minutes.

5| The foie will be loose in the cloth. Make it compact again by compressing it in a second cloth (leaving the first one on). Roll it as tightly as possible. Twist and tie the ends of the towel with a string and hang the torchon from a shelf in the refrigerator overnight.

Day 4:
Unwrap, slice and serve, or slice, cut with a ring mold, and serve.

Recipe courtesy of food writer Michael Ruhlman

Pickled Leeks (Yield: 3 cups)
Ingredients:

> 1 cup raspberries, cut in half
> 1 1/2 cups champagne vinegar
> 1 cup water
> 3 sprigs thyme
> 2 cloves
> 2 allspice berries
> 3 bay leaves
> Zest and juice of 1 lemon
> 1 teaspoon kosher salt
> 4 leeks, cleaned, cut in half, trimmed using the light green and white portions only, sliced into ¼ inch pieces

Directions:
1| In a small sauce pot, combine the vinegar with the water, thyme, cloves, allspice, bay leaves, lemon zest, lemon juice, and salt. Bring to a boil. Add the leeks, cover and simmer over medium heat for 2 minutes. Then add the raspberries.

2| Remove the sauce pot from the heat and let mixture cool completely. Transfer to a lidded container and refrigerate until needed. This pickle will keep for 2 weeks in a sealed container in the refrigerator.

Assembly of Dish:
1 loaf brioche

Slice brioche into 1/4-inch slices. Then using a quarter sized circle cookie cutter cut rounds out of the bread. Place the rounds on a cookie sheet and carefully toast in a 400° oven until golden brown. Allow the brioche rounds to cool.

Slice torchon and place on top of the brioche. Top with pickled leeks.

Savory Gougères
Filled with Mornay Sauce & Local Cheese
CHEF POLCYN | YIELD: 4 DOZEN

Ingredients:

> 1 cup skim milk
> 6 tablespoons butter
> 1 teaspoon salt
> 5 3/4 ounces all-purpose flour
> 4 large eggs

Directions:
1| Preheat oven to 425°.

2| In a sauce pot bring the milk, butter, and salt to a boil. Whisk in the flour and remove from heat. Work mixture together and return to heat. Continue working the mixture until all flour is incorporated and dough forms a ball.

3| Transfer mixture into bowl of a 5-quart standing mixer with a paddle attachment. Let it cool for a few minutes.

4| Begin to paddle the mixture at the lowest speed and add the eggs one at a time, making sure the first egg is completely incorporated before adding in the next egg. You should end up with a smooth dough.

5| Prepare a piping bag with a round tip and deposit the dough into the bag. Quickly begin to pipe golf ball-sized rounds about 2 inches apart onto parchment lined sheet pans.

6| Cook for 10-12 minutes, then reduce the temperature to 350°. Bake for 10 more minutes or until golden brown.

Mornay Sauce (Yield: 2 cups)

Ingredients:

2 1/2 tablespoons unsalted butter

3 tablespoons all-purpose flour

2 cups milk

1/4 teaspoon salt

1/8 teaspoon white pepper

Pinch nutmeg

2 ounces grated Gruyere cheese, or other local alpine cheese

Directions:

1| In a medium sauce pot over medium-high heat, melt the butter and add flour. Cook, and be sure to stir constantly until the roux is pale yellow and frothy, this should take about a minute or two. Be sure to stir constantly. Do not allow the roux to turn brown or this will discolor your sauce.

2| Begin to slowly whisk in the milk to the roux, and continue to whisk until the sauce begins to thicken. Bring the sauce to a boil then reduce to a simmer. Season the sauce with the salt, pepper, and nutmeg. Simmer for 2-3 more minutes. Now add in the grated cheese and whisk until melted.

Assembly of Dish:

Place the Mornay sauce into a piping bag that is fitted with a small round pastry tip.

Poke a small hole with a knife on the flat bottom of the gougère, then proceed to fill the gougère with the Mornay sauce. Repeat until all the gougères are full.

Before serving place the filled gougères on a sheet tray lined with parchment paper. Heat for 5 minutes in a 375° oven. Serve warm.

Duck Fat Popcorn
with Gin Cure Salt
CHEF MEYER | YIELD: 4 QUARTS

Ingredients:

3 ounces duck confit fat, warmed until melted (recipe in What the Duck*#%!, pg. 89)

1/2 cup popcorn

1 tea gin curing salt, (recipe in What the Duck*#%!, pg. 89)

Directions:

1| Place 2 ounces of fat and popcorn kernels in a heavy bottom pot. Cover with lid, place on medium heat burner and move back and forth until popcorn starts to pop.

2| Continue motion until you hear seeds slow dramatically in popping. Immediately transfer from heat to a large bowl and toss. You must release the steam or popcorn will get tough. Drizzle remaining duck fat onto popcorn and season with gin cure.

Chef Casadei

TRE MONTI RISTORANTE

Executive Chef Mark Casadei's interest in cooking began at a very young age, making pasta with his nonna, a San Marinese immigrant. He attended Northern Michigan University, graduating at the top of his class with a Bachelor's degree in Hospitality Management. He's delved into a number of different cuisines over the past 18 years, eventually choosing to specialize in Italian.

Casadei has been with Tre Monti Ristorante for the past six years. He places great emphasis on utilizing quality ingredients and putting a modern twist on classic dishes. He's also had the pleasure of collaborating with a number of award-winning chefs, including Francesco Straface of Rome, Italy.

Chef Chan

HONG HUA FINE CHINESE DINING

Chef Peter Chan and his partners established Hong Hua Fine Chinese Dining 14 years ago after an established career in Montreal, Canada. Within three years of opening, Hong Hua was selected as *Hour Detroit's* Restaurant of the Year in 2003, under the direction of Chan. Chan has received many awards and recognition, both nationally and in Southeast Michigan, including being selected as one of the top 10 Chinese chefs in the U.S.

Chicken Chicken

with Cracklin, Liver & Compressed Apple

CHEF RIGATO | YIELD: 20

Ingredients:

20 chicken skins, pressed, fried, laid flat
1 Granny Smith apple
Salt and pepper, to taste

Chicken Liver Mousse Ingredients:

2 tablespoons butter
2 cups chopped onion
1 cup chopped tart apple
1 teaspoon chopped fresh thyme leaves
1 pound chicken livers, cleaned
1/4 teaspoon ground white pepper
1/2 teaspoon salt
1/4 cup brandy
1 cup heavy cream

To Prepare Chicken Skins:

1| Bake chicken skins between two sheet trays lined with parchment paper at 350° for 30 minutes, until crispy. Season with salt and pepper.

2| Slice the apple, and use a vacuum package to compress.

To Prepare Mousse:

1| In a large sauté pan over low heat, melt the butter and cook onion, apple, and thyme, covered, until apples soften. Remove lid and increase heat to medium. Add the livers and cook until firm and still pink inside. Remove from the heat and allow to cool. Add the pepper, salt, and brandy and purée in a food processor; then chill, covered. Meanwhile whip the heavy cream to medium peaks. Fold into cooled, puréed liver mixture. Serve chilled on top of chicken skins along with a thin slice of apple.

Croque Madame
Topped with Quail Eggs

CHEF CONSTANTINE | SERVES: 6

Ingredients:

3 tablespoons unsalted butter

3 tablespoons flour

2 cups milk

12 ounces Gruyère, grated

1/2 cup Parmesan cheese, finely grated

Kosher salt and freshly ground
 black pepper, to taste

Freshly grated nutmeg, to taste

1 tablespoon chopped thyme

12 slices Pullman bread, 3/4-inch-thick,
 toasted

6 tablespoons Dijon mustard

12 thin slices baked ham

2 tablespoons canola oil

6 Quail eggs

Directions:

1| Heat butter in a 2-quart saucepan over medium-high heat. Add flour and cook, whisking, until smooth, about 1 minute.

2| Whisk in milk, and bring to a boil; reduce heat to medium-low. Let simmer until slightly reduced and thickened, 6–8 minutes.

3| Add ½ cup grated Gruyère and the Parmesan, whisk until smooth. Season with salt, pepper, thyme, and nutmeg.

4| Heat broiler to high. Place 6 slices of bread on a parchment-lined baking sheet, and spread 1 tablespoon mustard over each.

5| Top each with 2 slices of ham and remaining Gruyère. Broil until cheese begins to melt, 1–2 minutes. Top with remaining bread slices, then pour a generous amount of béchamel on top of each sandwich. Broil until cheese sauce is bubbling and evenly browned, about 3-4 minutes.

6| Meanwhile, make the fried eggs by heating oil in a 12-inch nonstick skillet over medium heat. Add eggs, season with salt and pepper, and cook until whites are cooked but yolks are still runny, about 3 minutes. Place an egg on top of each sandwich.

Curried Chicken Satay
with Hoisin Sauce Glaze

CHEF SOMERVILLE | SERVES: 4

Ingredients:

1 chicken, broken down into breast
 and thigh pieces, cut and skewered on
 to bamboo skewers

Sea salt, freshly ground black pepper,
 to taste

1 cup hoisin sauce

"Genghis Khan" Marinade:

1 cup onions, chopped

2 tablespoons garlic, chopped

3 tablespoons lemon juice

1/2 cup honey

3 tablespoons madras curry powder

1 1/2 teaspoons cayenne pepper, ground

2 teaspoons Colman's mustard powder

2 teaspoons black pepper, ground

1 cup water

Directions:

1| Combine all marinade ingredients in a food processor. Process until smooth.

2| Place chicken skewers in marinade overnight and up to 3 days. Use a gallon freezer bag to store marinade in.

3| Remove chicken skewers from marinade and season with salt and pepper. Place on preheated grill or cast iron skillet if doing indoors. Let brown slightly on one side before flipping.

4| Chicken should be just done and juicy at approximately 2-3 minutes.

5| Using a pastry brush glaze chicken with hoisin sauce and return to grill or oven until glaze is hot.

'Steak Frites' Gaufrette

Piedmontese Short Rib & Horseradish Tarragon Aioli

CHEF POLISEI | SERVES: 6

Ingredients:

1, 12-ounce baking potato, like russet, peeled, submerged in water

6 cups vegetable oil, for frying

1/4 teaspoon salt

Braised short ribs

Cabernet Jus

Tarragon Aioli:

1/2 cup mayonnaise

1 teaspoon finely grated lemon zest

1-2 tablespoons fresh lemon juice

1 teaspoon Dijon mustard

1 clove garlic, minced

Coarse salt and freshly ground black pepper, to taste

2 tablespoons of fresh chopped tarragon

Directions:

1| In a small bowl, place mayonnaise, lemon zest, lemon juice, mustard, and minced garlic. Season with salt and pepper. Stir to combine. Set aside.

2| To make the gaufrette potatoes, adjust a mandoline so the ridged blade is exposed by about 1/8 inch.

3| Remove the potato from the water and pat dry with a paper towel. Hold the potato at an angle of 45°, and slice potato over a mandoline. Turn the potato sideways, 45° in the opposite direction. This will make your first waffle-cut potato slice. Repeat the process, turning the potato after each pass over the blade to maintain the waffle-cut.

4| Place the potato slices in cold water to keep them from oxidizing.

5| Heat oil to 350° in a 1 gallon pot.

6| Working in batches, add potato slices a few at a time to the hot oil. Turn occasionally to ensure even browning. Cook until golden brown and crispy, about 3-4 minutes.

7| Using a slotted spoon or strainer, remove the chips from the oil. Place on a paper-lined plate and sprinkle with salt.

Braised Short Ribs

Ingredients:

2 pounds boneless short rib meat

1 tablespoon olive oil

1 tablespoon garlic, minced

1 tablespoon shallots, minced

1 tablespoon rosemary, freshly minced

1 tablespoon salt and pepper

1/2 of 1 onion, coarsely chopped

1/2 of 1 celery head, chopped

1 carrot, chopped

1/2 cup red wine

1 quart veal stock

Directions:

1| Coat beef evenly with olive oil, garlic, shallots, rosemary, salt, and pepper.

2| Place short ribs in a container and place it in refrigerator to marinate overnight.

3| The next day scrape off excess garlic, shallots, and rosemary.

4| Sear ribs on high heat on flat top until browned.

5| Remove ribs and reduce heat to medium. Add vegetables and caramelize for 10-15 minutes.

6| Deglaze pan with red wine. Add the stock and bring to a simmer.

7| Add ribs and cover with foil. Braise in a 350° oven for 4 hours.

8| Pull short ribs until shredded and toss in cabernet jus (see below). Salt until well seasoned, to taste.

Cabernet Jus

Ingredients:

- 1 1/2 cups red wine
- 2 tablespoons shallots, sliced
- 1 bay leaf
- 1 sprig of thyme
- 2 black pepper corns
- 3 1/2 cups reduced veal stock
- Brown sugar, to taste
- Kosher salt, to taste
- Ground white pepper, to taste
- Arrow root, as needed
- Water, as needed

Directions:

1| Combine red wine, shallots, bay leaf, thyme, and peppercorns in a sauce pot. Reduce by half, then add to the stock.

2| Reduce stock and wine mixture by half.

3| Slurry as needed with arrowroot. Season with salt, white pepper, and brown sugar. Strain through a chinois strainer.

Assembly of Dish:

Micro tarragon or fresh tarragon leaves

Place 1 tablespoon of shredded short rib on top of crispy gaufrette. Place ½ teaspoon of tarragon aioli on top of short rib. Garnish with one piece of micro tarragon or fresh tarragon on top of aioli.

Vitello Tonne

Seared Veal Tenderloin, Ahi Tuna Sashimi & Anchovy Caper Sauce

CHEF CASADEI | SERVES: 6-8

Cured Tuna:

- 1 lemon
- 1 lime
- 1 orange
- 3/4 ounces fresh parsley
- 1 sprig fresh rosemary
- 1/4 ounce fresh thyme
- 1 tablespoon fresh dill
- 4 fresh sage leaves
- 1 cup coarse sea salt
- 3 tablespoons brown sugar
- 1 tablespoon pickling spice
- 1/2, 1 ahi tuna, trimmed to cylinder shape, 1 inch x 5 inches long

Directions:

1| Remove zest from lemon, lime, and orange. Combine all zest in mixing bowl.

2| Chop all herbs and mix together with citrus zests.

3| Put sea salt, brown sugar, and pickle spice in food processor. Pulse a few times to combine. Add herb/zest mixture. Process until well mixed and homogenous.

4| Place salt mixture on tea towel, with tuna cylinder on top of salt. Roll tuna and salt together in tea towel, ensuring that all parts of tuna are in contact with the salt.

5| Place tuna roll over a sheet pan with a drying rack and refrigerate 8-10 hours.

6| Remove cured tuna from tea towel, discard salt, and rinse well under cold water. Dry well with paper towel and refrigerate until ready to use.

Tuna Sauce

Ingredients:

- 1 egg yolk
- 1/2 cup extra-virgin olive oil
- 2 teaspoons fresh lemon Juice
- 2 hard-boiled egg yolks
- 4 anchovy fillets
- 2 tablespoons capers, drained
- 1/2 cup canned tuna

Directions:

1| In small bowl, beat egg yolk with a hand mixer.

2| While mixing, add olive oil in a very thin stream to start emulsion. Add lemon juice a few drops at a time until fully incorporated. Set aside.

3| Add boiled egg yolks, anchovy, capers, and tuna to food processor. Pulse a few times to mix. Add mayonnaise created in first step to food processor and process until smooth. If extra seasoning is necessary, caper brine can be added as needed. Refrigerate in airtight container for up to 5 days.

Vitello Tonne

Ingredients:

- 1 veal tenderloin
- 1 cured tuna
- Salt and pepper, to taste
- 1 tuna sauce, see above
- Parsley
- Capers

Directions:

1| Trim veal of all fat and silver skin. With 6-inch or longer boning knife, pierce tenderloin lengthwise, through center of loin.

2| Make several small cuts inside center to open a hole extending all the way through the loin. Be careful not to break the cylinder.

3| Stuff cured tuna into the center of the veal tenderloin. Trim the ends of the loin for a neat appearance. Tie as roast to ensure even cylindrical shape.

4| Season lightly with salt and pepper and sear in preheated non-stick skillet over medium-high heat.

5| Turn veal for even sear all the way around, about 8-10 minutes. Veal should be light pink where it touches the tuna, with the tuna piece still raw.

6| Slice cooked veal/tuna roll into 6-8 even slices. Spread 1-2 ounces of tuna sauce on small plate and place veal/tuna slice on top of sauce. Garnish with parsley leaves and capers.

Atlantic Salmon Mousse
On Cucumber Wheel

CHEF DELL' ACQUA | SERVES: 12

Ingredients:

- 1 pound salmon fillet, skin off
- 1 teaspoon extra-virgin olive oil
- Salt and freshly ground black pepper
- 1 cucumber, sliced

For the Mousse:

- 1 pound soft cream cheese
- 1/4 cup brandy
- 1 lemon, zested and juiced
- Salt and freshly ground pepper, to taste

Directions:

1| Preheat the oven to 375°.

2| Season salmon fillet with olive oil, salt, and pepper.

3| Place on a baking sheet and bake until cooked through, about 10-12 minutes.

4| Remove from the oven and cool completely. Let chill for at least 30 minutes.

5| For the mousse, put the chilled salmon fillet in a food processor. Add all other ingredients and blend until smooth. Season with salt and pepper, to taste.

6| Using a pastry bag, pipe the mousse onto a cucumber wheel. Garnish with sliced smoked salmon, fresh dill, and caviar.

Chef Constantine

GREAT LAKES CULINARY CENTER

Originally from Detroit, Executive Chef Reva Constantine was lured into the culinary world when her passion for this industry and food was recognized at an early age. While in high school, Constantine went on to study culinary arts at Breithaupt Vocational Center in Detroit. There she found her true love, the culinary arts, and decided to become a professional chef.

After graduation she enrolled in the culinary arts program at Schoolcraft College. While in college she received her first opportunity to work in the industry at the Ritz Carlton Hotel in Dearborn as the employee café cook. Excited to have the chance to work with such talented chefs, she began moving her way up the culinary ladder. After a great experience at Schoolcraft College, Constantine decided to join the culinary competition team. She was elected team captain, and took her team all the way to nationals in Las Vegas where they won the national title.

Chef Constantine has won numerous awards for culinary competitions and worked as executive chef at great establishments such as Villa Maria in West Bloomfield, Gravity Bar and Grill in Milford, and Joe's Produce Gourmet Market in Livonia. Constantine is passionate about her position as executive chef at Great Lakes Culinary Center; she calls it her culinary playground.

Outside of creating culinary masterpieces around metro Detroit, 36-year-old Constantine enjoys spending time with her husband, Patrick, and their two children, Jaiden and Jeremiah.

Chef Del Signore

BACCO RISTORANTE

Like many chefs, Luciano Del Signore had a love affair with food from a very early age. Born in Garden City to immigrant parents from the Italian region of Abruzzo, Luciano had two things ingrained in him from a young age: a passion and appreciation for Italian food, and a work ethic characteristic of a different era.

His father Giovanni started Del Signore on his culinary path when he opened two Italian specialty grocers and a trattoria-style Italian restaurant, Fonte d'Amore, in Livonia in 1974. Gravitating toward the restaurant, Del Signore began as a busboy and dishwasher before moving onto waiting tables, and eventually working in the kitchen at 15 years old.

After graduating from high school, Del Signore ventured to Italy, and spent six months working in restaurants in Sulmona and Roccaraso. This experience shaped his entire philosophy and approach to Italian cooking. Once he returned home, he enrolled in the culinary arts program at Schoolcraft College, while simultaneously running the kitchen fulltime at Fonte d'Amore. After years of running the family restaurant, Del Signore opened the doors to his own Bacco Ristorante in 2002, consequently closing Fonte d'Amore.

In June 2010, Del Signore opened Bigalora Wood Fired Cucina, applying his philosophy of using quality ingredients, simple preparation, and balanced flavors. This restaurant is known for its authentic "pizza napoletana" cooked to perfection in a wood-burning oven.

Today, you'll see no signs of Del Signore slowing down. He's on his fourth restaurant and splits his time between Bacco and Bigalora, staying involved in nearly every facet of the business. He resides in Bloomfield Hills, with his wife Monica and their three children.

Miniature Lobster Rolls

with Saffron Orange Aioli

CHEF HALBERG | SERVES: 16

Ingredients:

4, 1 1/2 pound cooked lobsters, or 4 lobster tails, or 1 1/2 pounds lobster meat

Saffron orange aioli

3 tablespoons freshly squeezed lemon juice

2 inner celery stalks and leaves, finely chopped

2 tablespoons fresh parsley leaves, chopped

Salt and freshly ground black pepper, to taste

16 mini rolls, split and lightly toasted
Melted butter, for brushing

Directions:

1| Remove meat from the lobsters, chopping any large chunks into bite-size pieces.

2| In a bowl, combine the lobster meat, aioli, lemon juice, celery, parsley, and salt and pepper. Place lobster salad in refrigerator for 5 to 10 minutes.

3| Brush the rolls with melted butter and fill with the lobster salad.

Saffron Orange Aioli
Ingredients:

1/8 teaspoon saffron threads, crumbled
1 tablespoon hot water
1 garlic clove, chopped
1 teaspoon fresh orange zest, finely grated
1/4 cup fresh orange juice
1 tablespoon fresh lemon juice
3/4 teaspoon salt
1/4 teaspoon black pepper
1 large egg yolk
3/4 cup olive oil

Directions:

1| Stir together saffron and water in a small bowl until saffron begins to dissolve.

2| Transfer saffron mixture to a food processor along with remaining ingredients except oil. Pulse until combined.

3| With motor running, add oil in a thin, steady stream until aioli is thickened and emulsified. Transfer to a bowl and chill, covered, until ready to use.

■

Bliss Smoked Steelhead Roe
with Cantaloupe Gelee, Crème Fraîche, Celery, Cucumber & Black Pepper

CHEF MEYER | SERVES: 12

Ingredients:

1 ounce Bliss smoked steelhead roe
2 ounces whipped crème fraîche, seasoned with salt and freshly ground black pepper
1/2 of 1 English cucumber (use Parisian scoop to get balls)
12 celery leaves, yellow ones from the heart of the stalk
12 cantaloupe gelee shapes, (see below)
Freshly ground black pepper, to taste

Directions:

1| Pipe crème fraîche into basin of spoon.

2| Add smoked steelhead roe. Set cucumber and gelee to either side to accent. Garnish with celery leaf and black pepper.

Cantaloupe Gelee
Ingredients:

4 sheets gelatin
1 cup fresh cantaloupe juice
Sugar, to taste
Salt, to taste

Directions:

1| Bloom gelatin sheets in cold water for 10 minutes.

2| Bring cantaloupe juice to a simmer in a separate pot; don't boil. Adjust seasoning with salt and sugar.

3| Wring out gelatin and whisk it into warm juice until dissolved. Do this off the heat. Strain. Pour into vessel lined with plastic wrap. Cool in refrigerator.

4| Lift plastic out of vessel and transfer to cutting board. Cut into the shape you wish.

■

Beef Short Rib
on English Pea Purée

CHEF GROSZ | SERVES: 4

Ingredients:

4 –12 ounces beef short ribs
1 quart beef or chicken stock
2 ounces soy sauce
2 ounces honey
1 teaspoon chopped thyme
1 teaspoon chopped rosemary
1/2 teaspoon chopped garlic
1 cup fresh pea purée

Directions:

1| Braise short ribs covered with all ingredients at 300° until tender. About 3 hours. Serve on top of pea purée.

1| Duck Fat Detroit Popcorn with Gin Salt. *Chef Meyer.*

2| Steak Frites. *Chef Polisei.*

3| Mousse di Salmone con Centriolo. *Chef Dell'Acqua.*

4| Croque Madame topped with Quail Eggs.
   Chef Constantine.

1

3

4

Chef Gilbert

MARAIS

David Gilbert is a Michigan-raised chef who has an impressive work history and more than 23 years of experience in the culinary world. The nationally recognized chef is known for his creativity and culinary talents as the visionary behind some of Detroit's most acclaimed restaurants. He's worked at some of the most lauded restaurants in both the United States and Europe, such as the French Laundry (Yountville, Calif.), L'Astrance (Paris, France), Martine Berastegui (San Sebastian, Spain), and Michel Bras (Laguiole, France).

Gilbert moved back to Michigan in 2005 to take the position as chef at Rugby Grill in Birmingham, and in 2008, he took the helm at The Forest Grill in Birmingham as executive chef. In 2014, Gilbert opened his own restaurant, Marais, and in that same year was awarded *Hour Detroit's* restaurant of the year. Gilbert is owner and executive chef and his wife, Monica, is general manager; together the pair created a contemporary, French-based, modern haute cuisine menu.

Gilbert's extensive knowledge and experiences in nouvelle French and traditional French cuisine make him an ideal leader in Detroit's culinary industry. Working at numerous three-star Michelin-rated restaurants in Europe, and highly rated American restaurants has given him his devotion to culinary excellence.

Chef Green

COACH INSIGNIA

Born and raised in the Detroit area, Kevin Green is a graduate from the acclaimed culinary program at Schoolcraft College. He began his career at Rocky's of Northville as a line cook, and when the opportunity arose, he moved to the Hyatt Regency Dearborn as a sous chef working under Certified Executive Chef Tom Murray. In 2004 he advanced to Cuisine restaurant, as chef de cuisine, working closely with Certified Executive Chef Paul Grosz.

In 2008, Green joined the exceptional culinary team at Coach Insignia as chef de cuisine, where he continues to produce culinary innovations as executive chef. Green draws from local resources and markets as inspiration for his culinary presentations. Most recently Green has partnered with Whole Foods to design a monthly cooking exhibition, and branded the flagship Atwater in the Park. He continues to reside in the Detroit area with his wife and two children.

*Roasted Skuna Bay Salmon,
Recipe on page 100.*

Entrées

Black Cod

with Butternut Squash Tortelloni & Sage Brown Butter

CHEF POLISEI | SERVES: 4

Black Cod
Ingredients:

4, 4 ounce fillets of black cod

1 cup white wine

1/2 cup extra-virgin olive oil

Salt to season fish

8 pieces of butternut squash tortelloni

8 ounces sage brown butter

Butternut Squash Purée
Ingredients:

1 butternut squash

2 tablespoons softened butter

1/8 teaspoon orange zest

1 tablespoon honey

1/8 teaspoon ground cinnamon

1/8 teaspoon ground nutmeg

1/8 teaspoon allspice

1/8 teaspoon cayenne pepper

Salt and pepper, to taste

3 egg yolks

Directions:

1| Preheat oven to 400°.

2| Season black cod with salt, and place on baking sheet with white wine and olive oil.

3| Place in oven. The fish should not be fully submerged in the liquid. Cook fish for 8-10 minutes or until cooked.

4| Halve the squash lengthwise and remove seeds and strings. Rub the squash with softened butter. Season with salt and pepper.

5| Roast in 350° oven for 30-40 minutes or until fork tender.

6| Remove squash from the oven, scoop out the flesh and place in a blender or food processor.

7| Add remaining ingredients and purée until smooth.

8| For a smoother texture add heavy cream or more butter, and finish by putting through a fine mesh chinois.

Fresh Tortelloni

Ingredients:

- 3 cups all-purpose flour
- 2 large eggs
- 3 tablespoons water
- 1 teaspoon olive oil
- 1/2 teaspoon salt

Directions:

1| On a clean surface make a well with the flour.

2| In a measuring cup mix the eggs, water, oil, and salt. Pour the wet mixture slowly into the flour, and mix with your two fingers until all of the wet is incorporated.

3| If you are going to use a pasta machine to roll out the dough, at this point form the dough into a disk and cover with plastic wrap. Place in the refrigerator for 1 hour to rest.

4| If you are going to roll this by hand you should knead the dough on a floured work surface for 8-10 minutes.

5| Cut into 5-6 inch rounds with a round cookie cutter. Place 1-2 tablespoons of squash purée into the center of each round. Brush egg wash on the bottom half of the round, and fold over to seal.

6| Fold back around your finger and turn down the edge to form a tortelloni.

7| In rapidly boiling salted water add the tortelloni in batches. Cook for 3-5 minutes, or until they float to the surface. Remove to a strainer to drain.

Assembly of Dish:

- 4 tablespoons Marcona almonds
- 8 pieces fried sage leaves
- 2 tablespoons of channel zested lemon
- Fresh black truffle

On a large round dinner plate place fish at 6 o'clock and cooked tortelloni at 1 and 9 o'clock. Spoon desired amount of sauce on the plate, trying to keep sauce off of the fish. Garnish plate with marcona almonds, fried sage, and lemon zest. Shave fresh black truffles over entire plate.

Pork Belly Confit

with Oyster Beignet, Sweet Corn Purée & Apple Chow-Chow

CHEF POLISEI | SERVES: 4

Pork Belly Confit

Ingredients:

- 2 1/2 pound slab of pork belly with skin
- 6 cups pork fat or lard
- 12 cloves of peeled garlic
- 5 whole shallots
- 3 bay leaf
- 5 sprigs of thyme
- 5 sprigs of rosemary
- 1/4 cup herb salt or sea salt
- Canola oil

Directions:

1| Preheat oven to 250°.

2| Choose an ovenproof pot that is only slightly larger than the pork belly and has a lid. Put the belly in the pot and cover with the lard. The lard should cover the pork by 1/2 to 3/4-inch.

3| Heat the pot over low heat until the lard registers 190°. Cover.

4| Transfer to the oven, and cook until the pork is tender, about 4 hours, but start checking after 3 hours. As the belly cooks, it will lose fat and shrink. As this happens it is best to transfer the meat and fat to a smaller pot.

5| Remove the pot from the oven and let it cool to room temperature. The belly can be refrigerated in its fat, but it's preferred to press it to compress the internal layers of connective tissue and force out some of the excess fat, resulting in better texture and appearance.

6| To press it, transfer it to a deep baking dish. Pour enough fat into the dish to just cover the belly. Cover with plastic wrap, top with a smaller baking dish, and weight it down with a brick. Refrigerate for at least 12 hours. Reserve the extra fat. Once it's been pressed, the pork belly can be refrigerated, covered by fat, for up to 1 week.

7| Remove the pot from the refrigerator and let sit in a warm spot to soften the fat for 2-3 hours. Soften the fat enough so you can scrape it from the belly while keeping the belly as cold as possible so it will be easier to slice.

8| Remove the pork belly from the fat. Wipe off any cooking fat that clings to the meat. Remove the skin and score the fat on the belly in a crosshatch pattern.

9| Slice it or cut it into squares. Let it sit at room temperature for 20-30 minutes before sautéing.

10| Preheat the oven to 350°.

11| Heat some canola oil in a large ovenproof frying pan over medium-high heat just until smoking. Put the pieces of belly fat-side-down in the skillet, reduce the heat to medium-low. Cook until excess fat is rendered and the fat side is browned, about 18 minutes. Pour off excess fat about halfway through the cooking.

12| When the pork is browned, transfer the pan to the oven to heat through, about 10 minutes. Remove from the oven. Sprinkle with gray salt, and glaze with pickled gastrique before serving.

Apple Chow-Chow
Ingredients:
> 1 Pink Lady apple, brunoise
> 1 green tomato, brunoise
> 1 red pepper, brunoise
> 1 jalapeno, seeded and ribbed, brunoise
> 1/2 red onion, brunoise
> 2 cups apple cider vinegar
> 1 cup water
> 1/2 cup sugar
> 1/4 cup salt
> 2 teaspoons pickling spice

Directions:
1| Cut vegetables 1/8 inch by 1/8 inch, brunoise.

2| Mix vinegar, water, sugar, salt and pickling spice in a sauce pot. Bring to a boil.

3| Put vegetable mixture in a mason jar. Pour hot liquid over and cover. It will take at least a week for this to develop the correct flavors.

Pickled Apple Gastrique
Ingredients:
> Pickling liquid from apple chow-chow
> 1/2 cup sugar
> 2 tablespoons honey

Directions:
1| Strain liquid from chow-chow into a sauce pot.

2| Add sugar and honey to the pickling liquid. Reduce until it coats the back of a spoon.

Smokey Corn Purée
Ingredients:
> 2 cups corn
> 1 cup cream
> 1/4 pound of butter
> 1 teaspoon paprika
> 1 teaspoon chili powder
> 1/2 teaspoon cayenne pepper
> 1 tablespoon honey
> Salt, to taste

Directions:

1| In a sauce pot cook corn until soft in cream and butter.

2| Put hot corn, cream, and butter mixture into a blender or food processor. Add spices and honey, and season with salt. There will be plenty of acid and sweetness from the other ingredients, so if you like spice add more.

Lemon Aioli

> 1/2 cup mayonnaise
> 1 teaspoon finely grated lemon zest
> 1-2 tablespoons fresh lemon juice
> 1 teaspoon Dijon mustard
> 1 clove garlic, minced
> Coarse salt and ground pepper

Directions:

1| In a small bowl, place mayonnaise, lemon zest, lemon juice, Dijon mustard, and minced garlic. Season with salt and pepper. Stir to combine.

Oyster Beignet

Ingredients:

> 1/2 cup onion, diced
> 1/2 cup celery, diced
> 1 cup corn
> 2 tablespoons butter
> 1 pinch cayenne
> 1 pinch #2 grind black pepper
> 4 teaspoons white pepper
> 1/2 cup milk
> 2 eggs, beaten
> 2 tablespoons scallions
> 1/4 cup semolina
> 1/2 cup Drake's flour mix
> 1 teaspoon baking powder
> 4 shucked oysters
> 1 clove garlic
> 1 tablespoon granulated sugar

Directions:

1| In a pan combine onions, celery, and corn with butter.

2| Add seasonings. Cook until vegetables are soft.

3| Place in refrigerator to chill.

4| Add milk, eggs, and scallions to vegetable mixture, and purée.

5| Fold in all other ingredients. If mixture seems too thick, add more milk, if it seems too thin, add more Drake's flour.

6| Dredge oyster in seasoned flour. Dip in beignet batter, and fry until golden brown.

7| Season oyster beignet with salt when removed from oil.

Assembly of Dish:

Place 2 ounces of corn purée at 9 o'clock on a round plate with a spoon. Place tip of spoon in the center of the purée and drag to 3 o'clock on the plate. Place glazed pork belly in the center of the corn purée at 9 o'clock. Place oyster beignet at 3 o'clock. Spoon 2 tablespoons of apple chow-chow on pork belly. Garnish chow-chow with your green of choice. With a spoon, put a teaspoon of lemon aioli on oyster beignet.

Pan-Roasted Breast of Indiana Duckling

CHEF POLCYN | SERVES: 4

Ingredients:

> 4 boneless whole duck breasts, about 1 1/2 pounds each
> Sea salt and freshly ground black pepper, to taste

Directions:

1| Season the duck breasts with salt and pepper.

2| In a large sauté pan over medium high heat place the duck breasts skin side down. Cook until the skin is crisp and golden, about 5 minutes. Make sure your pan is hot before you add the duck breasts. Turn over the breasts and continue cooking until medium-rare, about 7-8 minutes more. Internal temperature should read 135°.

3| Remove duck from the pan and allow to rest for 3-4 minutes. Slice as desired.

Roasted Duck Roulade:

Ingredients:

- 1 Pekin duck, about 4 pounds, skinned, boned, and sinews removed, liver reserved
- 4 ounces pork back fat, diced
- 1 tablespoon kosher salt
- 1 1/2 tablespoons white pepper
- 1 tablespoon vegetable oil
- 1 tablespoon shallots, minced
- 1 cup dry sherry
- 1 tablespoon minced fresh sage
- 2 tablespoons roasted garlic
- 8 ounces unsalted butter
- 1 cup diced onion
- 1 cup chopped carrots
- 1 1/2 tablespoons minced garlic
- 2 bay leaves
- 1 bunch fresh thyme
- Kosher salt and freshly ground black pepper

Directions:

1| Weigh the dark meat. You should have about 12 ounces. Add enough pork fat to equal a total of 1 pound. Refrigerate. Cut the duck breasts into large dices, and refrigerate.

2| Lay the duck skin on a plastic wrap–lined baking sheet, outside down, arranging it so there are no wrinkles. Freeze for 1 hour. Freeze all your blades and bowls before gathering and measuring the remaining ingredients.

3| Season the breast with salt and pepper. Heat the oil in a medium sauté pan over high heat. When it's almost smoking, add the diced breast and sauté until nicely browned on all sides, but still raw in the center. Remove and set aside to cool.

4| Add shallots to the pan and cook until translucent, about 1 minute. Deglaze with the sherry, scraping up the browned bits from the pan with a wooden spoon. Reduce until mixture is almost a paste. Transfer to a small bowl and refrigerate until chilled.

5| Using a meat grinder, combine the duck leg, thigh meat, and fat with the liver, and grind through the small die into the bowl of a standing mixer bowl set in ice. Add the sage, roasted garlic, salt and pepper, and the chilled reduction to mix on low speed. Use the paddle attachment for 1-2 minutes, just until well-combined (don't over mix, or the fat will become too hot). Fold in duck breast. Refrigerate.

6| Do a quenelle test to check the seasoning, and adjust if necessary.

7| Remove the skin from freezer and scrape off all excess fat being careful not to cut or tear the skin.

8| Place the duck mixture down the middle of the skin and roll up into a roulade. Tie each end securely with butcher's twine, making sure to pinch the skin to trap the filling. Tie one loop of string lengthwise to make it snug. Tie individual loops of string around it, as with a roast, to make a tight, uniform roulade. Season with salt and pepper. Preheat the oven to 325°.

9| In a large heavy skillet, melt butter over medium-high heat. Add the onion, carrots, garlic, herbs, salt, and pepper, and sauté until they become translucent.

10| Transfer the vegetables and cooking juices to a baking sheet or roasting pan. Spread out to make a bed the width and length of the roulade. Place the roulade on top, and cover loosely with buttered or oiled parchment paper (this deflects the heat and inhibits moisture loss).

11| Bake. Baste the roulade frequently with the butter and juices in the pan, until a thermometer inserted in the center reaches 140°, about 45 minutes to 1 hour.

12| Remove the parchment paper and raise the oven temperature to 375° to brown the skin. Continue roasting until the internal temperature reaches 150°, about 15 more minutes. Let the roulade rest for 15 minutes before slicing into 1-inch/2.5-centimeter slices.

Sautéed End of Season Corn

Ingredients:

> 4 ears of corn, cut the kernels off the cob
> 2 tablespoons butter
> Salt and black pepper to taste

Directions:

1| Place a medium sized sauté pan over medium low heat. Melt the butter then sauté the corn for 8-10 minutes.

2| Season with salt and pepper to taste.

Tomatoes, Caramelized Shallot Tart Charred Heirloom Tomatoes

Ingredients:

> 1 tablespoon extra-virgin olive oil
> 2 1/2 pints cherry tomatoes
> Salt and freshly ground pepper

Directions:

1| Heat a medium sized sauté pan over high heat until very hot, this should take about 5 minutes. Carefully pour in the olive oil and add the tomatoes.

2| Cook until the tomatoes are lightly charred and about to burst; about a few minutes. Season with salt and pepper and serve right away.

Caramelized Shallot Tart (8 Servings)

Ingredients:

> 8 ounces Pâté Brisée
> 20 large shallots
> 2 ounces butter

> 1 egg
> 1/2 cup heavy cream
> 1/2 cup Parmesan cheese

Directions:

1| Roll dough out to 1/8 inch thick in a circle larger than an 11-inch flan mold. Place the dough in the tart mold and blind bake in a 350° oven. Bake for 15-20 minutes or until evenly golden brown. Remove from the oven and allow to cool.

2| In a large sauté pan sweat the shallots over medium heat with the butter and cover with a lid. When the shallots become clear and completely soft, remove the lid. Turn the heat to high and stir constantly while the shallots begin to caramelize. When the shallots are a deep brown color remove them from the heat and allow to cool.

3| Combine the egg and cream in a small bowl. Then pour over the cooled caramelized shallots. Pull out the tart shell, place the onions in the shell and evenly distribute. Sprinkle the Parmesan cheese on top of the shallots. Bake in a 350° oven until the tart is set, about 20-30 minutes. Allow the tart to cool slightly before you cut it.

Pâté Brisée (Makes 6, 11-inch tart shells)

Ingredients:

> 1 pound butter, small dice, cold
> 1 pound flour
> 1 egg
> Water

Directions:

1| In a medium-sized mixing bowl combine the butter and flour. Press the butter into the flour until the butter and flour resemble small crumbs.

2| Place the egg in a 1 cup measure and then fill the rest of the cup with water. Lightly whisk the egg and the water; then pour into the butter flour mixture and begin to knead.

3| As soon as the dough takes shape, remove from the bowl place onto plastic wrap, cover, and allow it to chill for 30 minutes or longer.

Tortellini In Brodo di Cappone

Capon-Stuffed Pasta & Capon Broth

CHEF DEL SIGNORE | SERVES: 4

Filling

Ingredients:

- 5 ounces ground capon
- 5 ounces mortadella, finely minced
- 2 1/2 ounces prosciutto di parma, finely minced
- 4 1/2 ounces Parmigiano–Reggiano, grated
- 1 egg
- Ground nutmeg, to taste
- Kosher salt, to taste

Directions:

1| Combine the capon, mortadella, prosciutto, Parmigiano–Reggiano, egg, nutmeg, and salt in a large bowl. Mix until fully incorporated.

2| Run a knife through the meat mixture, mincing it as finely as possible. Put in a food processor until it has a pâté-like texture.

Tortellini:

Use your favorite tortellini recipe.

Capon Broth:

- 1 whole capon
- 1 medium leek
- 1 stalk celery
- 1 small carrot
- 12 egg whites
- 1 cup tomato paste
- 1 cup white wine
- 4 quarts chicken stock

Directions:

1| Put all ingredients in a stockpot. Bring to a boil, and simmer for 4 hours.

2| Strain and chill.

Roasted Sturgeon

with Crawfish, Fennel & Orange

CHEF GROSZ | SERVES: 8

Ingredients:

- 8, 6-ounce sturgeon fillets
- 1 pound crawfish meat
- 2 ounces whole butter
- 1 fennel bulb
- 1/2 cup sugar
- 1/2 cup water
- 2 ounces Pernod or Sambuca
- 1 cup orange juice
- 1 cup white wine
- 2 ounces heavy cream
- 1/4 pound unsalted butter

Directions:

1| Sear sturgeon in pan with olive oil.

2| Finish in 400° oven for about 6 minutes. Cook to medium-rare.

3| Heat crawfish in whole butter until warm.

4| Shave fennel. Add fennel, sugar, water, and liquor to a sauce pot. Simmer on medium, until tender.

5| Reduce orange juice and wine to a syrup consistency.

6| Then add cream, reduce by half. Turn heat to low. Whisk in unsalted butter. Serve right away.

Chef Grosz

THE STAND AND CUISINE RESTAURANTS

You could say Proprietor and Chef of Cuisine Restaurant, Paul Grosz, began his career when he was 6 years old. That's when he discovered not only could he bake, but that he enjoyed it. At age nine, he worked at a neighborhood donut shop cleaning up, not baking.

Eventually, Chef Grosz studied under the legendary French chef, Jean Banchet at Le Francais, outside of Chicago. He apprenticed in pastries and continued on through every station. He later traveled to France and continued learning at Le Cordon Bleu.

Grosz then returned to the United States and assisted his brother, chef and owner of the award-winning restaurant, Oceanique. He went on to help revitalize La Rotisserie at the Hyatt-Regency in Dearborn. The owners of The Whitney took notice, and he became their executive chef for the next 10 years.

Along the way Grosz and Cuisine have been honored with many awards, including Best Restaurant of the Year by *Detroit Free Press*, and Best French Restaurant by *The Detroit News*.

Most recently, the American Culinary Federation certified him as an executive chef. Grosz is also an adjunct culinary arts instructor at Schoolcraft College. He opened The Stand in Birmingham with partner John Kelly in September 2013. With his commitment to his restaurant and family of six, Grosz is still able to squeeze in a little amateur hockey on a rather high-level league.

Chef Halberg

LOCAL KITCHEN AND BAR

Rick Halberg is an award-winning chef who has applied his exceptional culinary creativity in the Detroit area for the past 35 years. He's been the force behind several highly regarded restaurants including R.I.K.'s in West Bloomfield, Emily's in Northville, and Tutto Bene in Farmington Hills.

As proprietor and chef at Emily's, Halberg was honored with the Golden Dish Award from *Esquire* magazine, featured twice in *Gourmet* magazine's Best American Restaurants supplement, and was a recipient of the highest awards from *Zagat*.

He has been critically acclaimed in the media and consistently been given four star ratings at his restaurants. Recently, Halberg directed the culinary services for Hiller's Market, a family-owned chain of seven Southeast Michigan supermarkets in where he was the innovator of quality take-home options. He also supervised and trained a staff of 18, while overseeing all purchasing and inventory for this department.

Halberg graduated from the Culinary Institute of America in 1977. He is 63 years old, married to Karen, and has two children, Emily and Andy.

Porchetta

with Sauce Gribiche, Field Arugula & Lemon

CHEF POLCYN | SERVES: 25

Porchetta Ingredients:

2 1/2 pounds pork belly, skin removed

1/2 pound pork tenderloin

1/8 cup lemon zest

1/8 cup orange zest

1/8 cup toasted fennel

1/8 cup chopped garlic

Salt and cracked black pepper, as needed

Sauce Gribiche (Yield: 2 cups) Ingredients:

6 large hard-cooked eggs

3 teaspoons Dijon mustard

2 tablespoon fresh lemon juice

4 teaspoons white wine vinegar

1 1/2 cup vegetable oil or canola oil

3 tablespoons chopped capers

6 tablespoons chopped cornichons

2 teaspoon minced fresh flat-leaf parsley

2 teaspoon minced fresh tarragon

2 teaspoon minced fresh chervil

Kosher salt and freshly ground black pepper

To Prepare Porchetta:

1| Preheat oven to 300°.

2| Lay the belly out, skin side down. Season liberally with salt and pepper.

3| In a small bowl combine the zests, fennel, and garlic then distribute this mixture all over the belly. Take the pork tenderloin and lay it down the center of the belly, longwise. Begin to roll the belly up longwise, like a jelly roll, and tie securely with butchers twine.

4| Place the rolled belly on a roasting pan and place in the oven. The belly will slowly roast for 8-10 hours or until fork tender. Another option is to sous vide the belly at 165° for 36 hours.

5| Remove from oven and chill overnight.

6| To serve the porchetta, slice paper thin and serve with arugula salad and sauce gribiche.

To Prepare Sauce Gribiche:

1| Separate the egg yolks from the whites. Press the yolks through a fine sieve into a medium bowl. Add the mustard, lemon juice, and vinegar and season with a healthy pinch of salt. Whisking continuously, drizzle in the oil, drop by drop at first, then in a very thin stream, until all the oil is incorporated and you have a smooth, thick emulsion.

2| Finely dice the egg whites and fold them into the sauce, along with the remaining ingredients. Taste and adjust the seasoning, adding more lemon juice and/or salt and pepper as necessary.

Guancia di Vitello Arrosto

Braised Veal Cheek, Polenta, Roasted Cipollini & Crispy Brussels Sprouts

CHEF DEL SIGNORE | SERVES: 16

Ingredients:

> 1/2 cup extra-virgin olive oil
> 2 pounds fresh veal cheeks, skinned
> 1 onion
> 1 carrot
> 2 ribs celery, diced
> 10 sage leaves
> 1 cup tomatoes, crushed
> 1 cup dry white wine
> 4 cups chicken stock
> Salt and pepper

Directions:

1| Season and sauté the veal cheeks in a shallow pot over medium-high heat with olive oil. Brown on both sides.

2| Remove veal, then add onion, carrots, celery, and sage, and sauté until caramelized.

3| Add veal back to pan, add tomatoes, wine, and stock. Bring to a simmer. Cover and bake at 375° for 2–2 1/2 hours, until tender. Remove and let cool. Remove cheeks, strain sauce, and reduce.

Roasted Cipollini Onions
Ingredients:

> 6 onions
> 1 teaspoon extra-virgin olive oil
> Salt and pepper, to taste

Polenta
Ingredients:

> 2 cups polenta flour
> 6 cups water
> Salt, to taste
> 1/4 cup extra-virgin olive oil

Directions:

1| Bring water to boil. Add polenta flour, salt, and olive oil. Simmer for 45 minutes.

Crispy Brussels Sprouts
Ingredients:

> 3 cups Brussels sprouts leaves
> 1/4 cup grated Parmesan
> 1 teaspoon red wine vinegar
> Salt and pepper, to taste

Directions:

1| Fry leaves until golden brown.

2| Toss in a bowl with Parmesan, vinegar, salt, and pepper.

Assembly of Dish:

Center polenta on plate. Place a veal cheek on top. Top with 1 1/2 ounces of sauce from veal preparation, and sprinkle. Garnish with onions and brussels sprouts.

Coriander-Crusted 'Big Eye' Tuna

with Haricots Verts, Fingerling Potatoes, Nicoise Olives & Chimichurri

CHEF WARD | SERVES: 4

Ingredients:

4, 4-ounce center cut "Big Eye" Hawaiian Ahi Tuna portions

Coriander spice mix

12 ounces fingerling potatoes, quartered

4 ounces haricots verts, cut in half diagonally

4 ounces nicoise olives, halved

Olive oil, for cooking

Tomato caper relish

Chimichurri sauce

Directions:

1| Encrust the tuna in the coriander spice mix and sear each side evenly for 15 seconds in a hot sauté pan with olive oil. Let rest.

2| In a separate pan, sauté the fingerling potatoes with olive oil until golden brown, and finish by adding the haricots verts and nicoise olives.

Coriander Spice Mix
Ingredients:

4 tablespoons whole coriander seeds, roasted

1 tablespoons whole black peppercorns

1 tablespoon sea salt

1 teaspoon sugar

1 pinch cumin

Directions:

1| With a spice blender, blend the coriander and black peppercorns separately, then mix together in a bowl.

Tomato Caper Relish
Ingredients:

2 large tomatoes, diced small

1 tablespoon capers

1 ounce shallot, minced

1 ounce olive oil

Lemon juice, to taste

Salt and white pepper, to taste

Directions:

1| Combine all ingredients.

Chimichurri Sauce
Ingredients:

1 bunch flat leaf parsley

1 bunch cilantro

1 ounce red wine vinegar

1 clove garlic, minced

1 pinch black pepper

1 pinch cayenne pepper

6 ounces olive oil

Directions:

1| Add all ingredients except for the olive oil into a blender. Turn it on and very slowly add the oil until a fluid emulsification forms.

Assembly of Dish:

Assemble the plate by using the potatoes, haricots verts and nicoise olives as a base in the middle. Slice the tuna into 5-6 thin pieces and layer over top. Garnish with the tomato caper relish, and spread the chimichurri sauce around the outside.

Dry Aged Colorado Rack of Lamb

with Truffle Polenta, Rapini Salsa Verde
& Port Wine Balsamic

CHEF CASADEI | SERVES: 6-8

Lamb Chop
Ingredients:

2 marinated lamb racks

1 ounce extra-virgin olive oil,
and more to finish

2 garlic cloves, crushed

2 cups port wine*

1 1/2 ounces balsamic vinegar

1/2 cup lamb stock

1 ounce butter, unsalted

Salt and pepper, to taste

Truffle polenta

Rapini pesto

Directions:

1| Preheat oven to 450°.

2| In preheated cast iron skillet, sear room-temperature lamb racks on both sides in olive oil. Remove lamb to a baking sheet lined with a drying rack and roast in the oven until internal temperature reads 125° for medium rare, about 20-30 minutes. Let it rest 10 minutes before carving.

3| Remove excess fat from skillet and add garlic. Sauté until it just begins to brown.

4| Remove skillet from heat. Add port wine to deglaze pan. Light alcohol vapor with a stick lighter, and allow alcohol to burn off. Return pan to heat, and reduce by half.

5| Add vinegar and stock; continue to reduce until light syrup forms. Remove from heat and whisk in cold butter. Strain and hold until needed. Season with salt and pepper.

6| In a nonstick skillet, sear polenta on both sides in olive oil over medium heat until a golden crust forms.

Rapini Pesto
Ingredients:

1 bunch rapini

2 ounces pistachio nuts

2 ounces Grana Padano, grated

1/2 cup extra-virgin olive oil

Salt and pepper, to taste

Directions:

1| Remove rapini leaves and discard stems. Blanch leaves in pot of boiling, salted water for 5 minutes. Drain and shock in ice water bath.

2| Pulse pistachio in food processor until mostly crushed.

3| Add drained rapini leaves and Grana Padano. Process on high speed to form paste. With machine running, add olive oil in thin stream to emulsify ingredients. Continue to process to desired consistency. Season with salt and pepper. This can be stored with a thin layer of olive oil on top for up to 6 days in the refrigerator. Before use, bring to room temperature and mix well to re-emulsify.

Lamb Chop Marinade
Ingredients:

2 lamb racks

1 cup light olive oil

2 tablespoons thyme, chopped

1/2 cup port wine*

1/4 cup balsamic vinegar

*preferred wine is Fonseca Porto Bin No. 27

Directions:

1| Trim lamb racks of excess fat and clean the bones by scraping them with the back edge of a paring knife.

2| Whisk together oil and thyme. While whisking add wine in a thin stream to emulsify. Do the same with the balsamic vinegar.

3| Season the lamb racks with salt and pepper. Place in suitable pan and cover lamb with marinade. Refrigerate 8-12 hours. After 8-12 hours, remove lamb from marinade and pat dry. Bring to room temperature before cooking.

White Truffle Polenta

Ingredients:

- 1 pound white cornmeal
- 4 cups chicken broth
- 1/2 cup heavy cream
- 1/2 ounce butter
- 2 teaspoons white truffle, shaved

Directions:

1| Combine cornmeal and broth in heavy bottomed pot and bring to a boil. Stir often with a wooden pasta fork.

2| Reduce heat to medium and stir continuously until polenta begins to pull away from side of pan, about 30-45 minutes.

3| Add cream and butter. Continue to stir continuously until polenta again pulls away from side of pan, about 10 minutes.

4| Remove from heat, stir in truffle, and pour into greased loaf pan. Smooth the surface and cool.

5| When cool, unmold polenta from loaf pan. Cut into 6-8 equal pieces. Store in airtight container in refrigerator for up to 3 days.

Assembly of Dish:

After resting 10 minutes, carve lamb by cutting between the rib bones into individual chops. Plate with truffle polenta and garnish with 1 ounce of port wine reduction and 1 ounce of rapini pesto.

Bricoche Crusted Walleye

with Mushroom Ragout

CHEF JOHNS | SERVES: 4

Ragout

Ingredients:

- 1 pound mixed mushrooms: shiitake, cremini, or oyster
- 4 tablespoons unsalted butter
- 1/2 cup small onion, chopped
- 1 tablespoon fresh thyme leaves
- 1 cup white wine
- 1 cup brown chicken stock, or mushroom stock
- Salt and pepper to taste

Directions:

1| Clean all the mushrooms and remove any stems or dry ends. Quarter all the mushrooms and put in a bowl.

2| Heat half of the butter in a large skillet over medium-high heat. Add mushrooms and spread them out evenly in the pan; increase the heat to high. Let the mushrooms cook undisturbed until they brown, then shake the pan to turn them over. Continue to cook until nicely browned, about 5 minutes.

3| Add the onion and cook until softened, about 2 minutes. Season the mushrooms with salt and pepper, and add the thyme.

4| Pull the pan off the heat and add wine. Return pan to the heat and scrape up any of the brown bits on the bottom of the pan with a wooden spoon. Add the stock and bring to a boil; reduce until thickened. Add the rest of the butter, and stir to incorporate. Remove from the heat and keep warm.

Walleye
Ingredients:

- 4, 7-ounce walleye fillets, skinned and pin boned
- Salt and pepper, to taste
- 2 tablespoons Dijon mustard
- 1/2 cup brioche or other soft, fresh breadcrumbs
- 4 tablespoons olive oil

Directions:

1| Preheat oven to 375°.

2| Season each fillet with salt and pepper. Brush each fillet, on one side only, with the mustard. Press each fillet, mustard side down, into the breadcrumbs to form even coat.

3| Heat oil in a large non-stick skillet over medium high heat. Carefully lay each fillet breadcrumb side down into the hot pan. Cook for 2 minutes, and place in oven to finish for 6-8 minutes.

4| Remove pan and carefully turn the walleye over to finish cooking on the other side.

Assembly of Dish:
Divide the ragout between 4 plates and top with the walleye, crust side up. Serve with roasted potatoes and wilted greens.

Sweet Pea Agnolotti
with Ramps, Morels & Burrata
CHEF HOLLYDAY | SERVES: 6

Ramps & Morels
Ingredients:

- 2 tablespoons unsalted butter
- 2 tablespoons olive oil
- 1 bunch of ramps (1/4 pound), washed, trimmed, cut to 2-inch lengths
- 1/2 pound morel mushrooms
- 2 ounces orange miso beurre blanc, see page 120

Directions:

1| Preheat medium sauté pan over medium-high heat. Add butter and olive oil. Once butter is sizzling, add trimmed ramps and sauté for 1 minute.

2| Add morels and turn heat down to medium. Gently cook until mushrooms are soft and a little liquid still remains. Set aside.

3| For the plating, use a bowl and place orange miso beurre blanc on the bottom. Add the crab cake. Heat asparagus and place on the cake, then put the halibut on the next layer. Garnish with the mushrooms and serve.

Sweet Pea Agnolotti
Ingredients:

- 2 shallots, minced
- 6 tablespoons unsalted butter
- 1 pound fresh sweet peas (blanched), or 1 pound frozen peas
- 1/4 cup mascarpone cheese
- Zest of 1 lemon
- 1/4 cup Parmesan cheese
- Salt and pepper, to taste
- 1 pound fresh pasta sheets
- Coarse cornmeal
- 1 Zingerman's burrata, 8 ounces, evenly divided into 6 portions
- High-quality olive oil
- 4 tablespoons unsalted butter
- Juice of 1/2 lemon

Directions:

1| In a medium sauté pan, melt 2 tablespoons of butter over medium heat. Add shallots. Cook for 2 minutes or until soft.

2| Add the peas and mascarpone cheese. Cook for 1 minute.

3| Scrape mixture into food processor with the lemon zest, Parmesan, salt, and pepper. Process until smooth. Taste for seasoning, cool down, and put in a pastry bag fitted with 1/2-inch tip.

4| Pull out one sheet of fresh pasta. Pipe a straight line of filling lengthwise on the pasta sheet, leaving enough pasta at the top to fold over the filling. Fold the pasta top over the filling. Press firmly to seal. Moisten the tip of your finger and run it along the seam if it doesn't want to stick together.

5| Use a wheeled pasta cutter or a sharp knife to cut the filled tube of pasta away from the rest of the sheet, making sure to keep the sealed strip intact. Use the tips of your fingers to pinch the tube of pasta into equally sized sections, creating a seal between pockets of filling.

6| Use the wheeled pasta cutter to separate the sections. Cut through each, leaning the tube of pasta in the direction you're cutting.

7| Place the finished agnolotti in a tray of coarse cornmeal. Repeat until all of the pasta sheets and filling have been used. At this point the pasta can be cooked right away, covered and refrigerated overnight, or frozen.

8| When ready to use, bring a large pot of water to boil. Salt water to taste like the sea. Add agnolotti. Cook for 2 minutes.

9| Remove cooked pasta and add to the mushroom mix, reserving 1/2 cup pasta water.

10| Bring the mixture to a simmer, adding bits of pasta water until it's saucy consistency. Add butter and lemon juice. Turn off heat. Stir until mixture is creamy.

Assembly of Dish:

Divide pasta and mushroom mixture evenly between six plates. Place an even amount of burrata on each dish. Finish with olive oil and serve.

Fennel & Hakurei Turnip Salad

with Fall Greens & Honey-White Vinaigrette

CHEF JOHNS | SERVES: 4

Ingredients:

> 1/2 pound Hakurei turnips or mild radishes, sliced very thin
> 1 medium bulb of fennel, sliced very thin, white part only
> 6 cups fall greens such as arugula, radicchio, or frisée

Dressing
Ingredients:

> 1 tablespoon Dijon mustard
> 1 teaspoon fresh garlic, minced
> 1/3 cup white wine vinegar
> 2/3 cup extra-virgin olive oil
> Salt and pepper, to taste

Directions:

1| For the dressing, place mustard, garlic, and vinegar in medium bowl. Slowly whisk in all of the oil until the dressing is emulsified. Season with salt and pepper.

2| In a small bowl, season turnip and fennel slices with salt and pepper. Toss with 2 tablespoons of dressing.

3| Arrange the vegetables in the center of 4 chilled plates. Add the greens to the bowl, season, and toss with 1/4 cup of the dressing. Top each pile of fennel and turnips with a handful of dressed greens.

FEATURED CHEF

Chef Hollyday

SELDEN STANDARD

Andy Hollyday is the co-owner and executive chef of Selden Standard, which opened in 2014. The *Detroit Free Press* named it Restaurant of the Year in 2015 for its menu that emphasizes a farm-to-table philosophy and wood-fired oven cooking techniques. Hollyday began his career 20 years ago, cooking at a small family restaurant in his hometown of Toledo. Prior to Selden Standard, he served as executive chef of Michael Symon's Roast where he was named Best Chef in 2012 by *Hour Detroit*. Prior to Roast, Hollyday cooked at the Ritz Carlton (Dearborn), L'Essentiel (Chambery, France), Tribute (Farmington Hills), and Oliveto (Oakland, Calif.), among others. He is a 2003 graduate of the Culinary Institute of America in Hyde Park, N.Y. A resident of Detroit, Hollyday spends most of his free time at the nearest coffee shop, his community garden, the Detroit Film Theater, and Comerica Park — and remains, despite his better judgment, a die-hard Lions fan.

Chef Meyer

IRIDESCENCE

Chef de Cuisine Benjamin Meyer is fluent in a wide array of culinary styles. His expertise in various facets of the culinary industry, coupled with his undeniable talent, make him a priceless asset inside Iridescence, a premier, AAA Four-Diamond dining destination, located on the top floor of MotorCity Casino Hotel.

Since his introduction, Meyer has made several drastic changes to Iridescence's dynamic menu, with his ability to enhance the personality and character of each dish, drawing inspiration from the beautiful ambience.

Prior to Iridescence, Meyer was executive chef of Chen Chow Brasserie, and assisted in the openings of both Michael Mina restaurants, Bourbon Steak and Saltwater. Both were once located in MGM Grand Detroit, where he was the executive sous chef and purchaser for both properties.

Previously, Meyer accelerated his craft with Chef Don Yamauchi as chef de cuisine at the well-known Tribute. He also worked with Chef Scott Mickelson of Paragon on the 24th floor of the Grand Pequot Tower at Foxwoods Resort Casino. Over the years he has worked at restaurants that have received many distinguished awards, including Four Diamond achievements, Restaurant of the Year, and *Wine Spectator* Awards.

Meyer holds a Bachelor of Applied Science in Culinary Arts degree from Johnson and Wales University where he graduated summa cum laude, along with an Associate's of Applied Science in Business Management from Washtenaw Community College. He's also completed course requirements for Thai cuisine from the Suan Dusit International Culinary School in Bangkok, and completed course requirements for Pan Asian Cuisine from At-Sunrice Culinary Academy in Singapore.

Cabernet Braised Beef Short Rib

with Vanilla-Ginger Sweet Potato Purée, Amaranth, Edamame, Walnut

CHEF MEYER | SERVES: 6-8

Ingredients:

5-pound bone-in beef short rib
Salt and pepper, to taste
3 carrots, chopped
2 Spanish onions, chopped
4 stalks of celery, chopped
1 bottle California cabernet sauvignon
2 cinnamon sticks
2 star anise
3 cloves
16 coriander seeds
6 sprigs fresh thyme
1 cup Hoisin sauce
4 cups chicken or veal stock
Neutral oil

Directions:

1| Heat a large pan on high with salt and pepper, and add oil to sear short rib on all sides.

2| Remove from pan and pour off excess oil, leaving about an ounce. Add carrot, onion, and celery to the hot pan, and let natural moisture of vegetables deglaze pan. When vegetables are fragrant and start to break down, add bottle of wine.

3| Reduce by half and scrape bottom of pan with wooden spoon. Add cinnamon, star anise, cloves, coriander, thyme, Hoisin. Bring to a simmer and stir.

4| Add stock and bring to a simmer. Place short ribs back in and cover with lid. Place in preheated 350° oven until tender, around 2 1/2-3 hours.

5| At this point let the short ribs rest out of the oven for 30 minutes. Remove the ribs to a clean pan, strain the braising liquid, and add strained liquid back to pan with short ribs. Allow short ribs to cool in braising liquid overnight.

6| Once cool, remove the bone with a sharp knife for cleaner presentation. On the day you plan to serve, reheat the short ribs in the strained braising liquid. Baste them with the sauce.

Sweet Potato Purée

Ingredients:

2 pounds large sweet potatoes

3-4 ounces heavy cream

1 vanilla bean, split and warmed in cream

2 ounces ginger, grated, and the juice squeezed through a towel or cheesecloth into a ramekin

Salt, to taste

Directions:

1| Place potatoes on a pan lined with salt. Poke holes with a fork into sweet potatoes and bake at 350° until they are cooked through.

2| Split cooked potatoes in half and transfer to food processor. Then add cream, vanilla bean, and ginger juice. Season with salt as needed.

3| Pass purée through a fine mesh strainer and reserve for plating warm.

Brûléed Scallops

Ingredients:

1/4 pound Nantucket bay scallops

Granulated sugar, to taste

Kosher salt, to taste

Directions:

1| Gently press on scallops with paper towel to get them as dry as possible.

2| Season cookie sheet with salt. Add scallops so they are not touching. Sprinkle them evenly with sugar. Brûlée them working back and forth, never staying in one spot too long. One side salty and one side bittersweet.

Assembly of Dish:

1/4 cup walnuts, toasted

1/4 cup fresh soybeans, gently warmed in water or steamed

Amaranth, optional

Make a clean stroke on the plate with the potato. Set short rib in the center of the stroke. Drizzle it with a little of braising liquid. Crush walnut over the top. Add the bruleed scallops and soybeans. Garnish with amaranth.

What The Duck*#%!

Maple Glazed Duck Breast Tasso, Apple Scented Duck Mousse, Duck Confit Spring Roll, Pumpernickel Toast, Frisee & Orange-Apple Gastrique

CHEF MEYER | SERVES: 6

This recipe has many components— make one or all of them.

Ingredients:

1 whole Culver duck, broken down into breasts and legs (Render the fat for confit, also used in popcorn, page 37)

1 gastrique batch

6 spring rolls

1 batch of duck mousse

2 duck tasso breasts, cut into 18 slices each

Duck Confit

Note: The confit is used in multiple components of this dish.

Ingredients:

- 2 duck leg quarters
- 1 pint duck fat, from what you rendered from breaking down the duck
- 1/2 cup gin cure:
- 3 ounces salt, 1/2 ounce sugar, 12 black peppercorns, 1/4 tea fennel seeds, 24 coriander seeds, 10 juniper berries, zest of 1 orange and 1 lime, 12 sprigs fresh thyme
  Place in food processor and process until all ingredients have married.

Directions:

1| Season both sides of the duck breast with gin cure liberally. Place on wire rack in refrigerator overnight.

2| Rinse breast and pat dry with towel. Place breasts in pan and cover with duck fat.

3| Cover pan with foil and put in 225° oven for 3 hours. Remove from oven, remove cover, and let sit on counter for 30 minutes. Refrigerate overnight.

4| The next day, gently heat pan to melt duck fat. Remove legs and pick meat. Reserve half for spring roll and half for mousse. Extra cure and final duck fat are used in the popcorn appetizer (see page 37).

Duck Spring Roll

Ingredients:

- 1/2 duck meat from confit recipe
- 1 teaspoon sambal chili sauce
- 1 ounce pea shoots or tendrils
- 1 ounce baby arugula
- 2 ounces carrot, julienne
- 6 spring roll wrappers

Directions:

1| Divide ingredients equally and roll standard spring rolls. Can be made in advance and frozen.

Duck Mousse

Ingredients:

- 1/2 duck meat from the confit recipe
- 4 ounces apple cider
- 4 ounces duck or chicken stock
- 2 ounces whipped cream, stiff peaks
- 1 ounce heavy whipping cream

Directions:

1| In sauce pot add cider and stock. Reduce to 1 ounce, and let cool to room temperature.

2| In a food processor add duck confit and reduction. Process until homogenous mixture is achieved. Add heavy cream and process until blended through. If you go too long, the cream will break or turn to butter.

3| Transfer contents to a clean bowl. Use a rubber spatula to fold in whipped cream. Refrigerate at least 1 hour to set up. Transfer to piping bag.

Duck Tasso

Ingredients:

- 1/3 cup sugar
- 2/3 cup kosher salt
- 2 duck breasts
- 1 ounce Michigan maple syrup
- Tasso rub:
- 1 teaspoon black pepper, 1 teaspoon marjoram, 1 teaspoon ground allspice, 1/2 teaspoon cayenne pepper

Directions:

1| Mix sugar and salt. Pack the duck breasts in it overnight. 24 hours later, rinse off with cold water and pat dry with a towel.

2| Rub tasso mix all over duck breast. Hot smoke duck for 15 minutes.

3| Transfer duck breast to heavy-bottomed skillet and set to low. Let duck breast sit until most of the fat from the skin is rendered out.

4| Place breast on baking sheet and bake in oven at 350° until internal temperature is 135°.

5| Remove from oven and brush duck breast with syrup. Let rest at least 30 minutes until it is room temperature. Wrap each breast individually in plastic wrap and refrigerate 24-48 hours.

Gastrique

Ingredients:

1 cup granulated sugar

1/2 cup cold water

1 cup orange juice

1 cup apple cider

2 ounces apple cider vinegar

Directions:

1| In one pot, add sugar and water. Cook sugar until it gets to amber stage.

2| In second pot, add both juices and reduce until you have 1/2 cup of liquid. Remove from heat and whisk in vinegar.

3| When sugar is at amber state remove from heat and place pot in sink. Whisk in the second pot of liquid. Be careful: use big pot because volume will increase up to 400 percent. If it doesn't all incorporate put back on burner and continue to whisk. If it's too thick you can add water, and if it's too thin, cook a little longer. Remember it will thicken as it cools. Keep sauce at room temperature; don't refrigerate.

Assembly of Dish:

Pumpernickel croutons

Frisee

On a linear plate, drizzle gastrique — it acts as sauce and holds everything in place. Starting from the left, place large crouton down and pipe mousse out of pastry bag or do a quenelle. In the center place a spring roll that has been cut in half on the bias and stack. On the right place 6 slices of duck tasso. Use small croutons as random garnish, using the gastrique as glue. Garnish with frisee.

Michigan Lamb Crudo

with Curried Squash & Naan

CHEF RIGATO | SERVES: 6

Ingredients:

2 pounds of all-natural lamb, trimmed and ground

1/2 cup preserved lemon

1 large onion, diced small

Salt and pepper, to taste

Olive oil and garlic oil, to taste

Directions:

1| Mix everything in a bowl and taste until satisfied. Serve chilled.

Curried Squash

Ingredients:

1 large Spanish onion, diced roughly

1/2 cup butter

5 tablespoons of Middle Eastern curry powder

1 kabocha squash, split, gutted, roasted until soft

1 cup chicken stock

Directions:

1| Sauté onion in butter until soft. Add curry until toasty.

2| Add squash and chicken stock. Lightly cook until squash is soft.

3| Purée in food processor, adjust seasoning until satisfied.

Naan Bread (20 2-ounce servings)

Ingredients:

> 1/2 teaspoon active dry yeast
>
> 1 pound, 8 ounces all-purpose flour
>
> 1 1/2 teaspoons salt
>
> 1 1/2 teaspoons sugar
>
> 1/4 cup milk
>
> 2 tablespoons olive oil
>
> 9 ounces water
>
> Butter to grease tray
>
> Flour to roll out dough

Directions:

1| Dissolve yeast in water, and put in bowl of stand mixer. Add all remaining ingredients. Mix dough with dough hook for 10 minutes on medium speed.

2| Place dough in a greased bowl and cover in a warm area. Allow to ferment for 2 hours.

3| Scale dough into 2-ounce portions and round into balls. Place balls onto greased tray and brush with olive oil. Cover and rest for 15 minutes, or place in refrigerator for later use.

4| Roll out dough on a well-floured surface. Roll as thin as possible. Place on tray lined with parchment paper. Bake at 550°, until dough bubbles up and starts to brown.

Veal Medallion

with Gorgonzola Cheese, Grilled Polenta & Balsamic Vinaigrette Sauce

CHEF DELL' ACQUA | SERVES: 6

Ingredients:

> 2 whole veal tenderloins
>
> Salt and pepper, to taste
>
> 1 tablespoon oil
>
> 1 bunch of rapini
>
> 4 ounces of caul fat
>
> 1 tablespoon flour
>
> 1 ounce Gorgonzola cheese

Directions:

1| Clean any fat from the veal. Cut the tenderloins lengthwise as a butterfly and tenderize to 1-inch thick. Season with salt and pepper.

2| Braise the rapini and stuff in the middle of the veal. Fold the veal over to close it. Wrap the fillet with caul fat, dust it with flour, and cook it on medium heat for 5 minutes.

3| Remove it from the heat, and bake it for 10 more minutes at 375°.

4| When ready cut it into 1 inch slices. Top with Gorgonzola cheese, and bake it until the cheese melts.

Assembly of Dish:

> Balsamic reduction, for plating
>
> 6 tomatoes, grilled
>
> Eggplant, sautéed
>
> Caramelized onion
>
> Veneto, yellow, and black taragna polenta

Serve on a plate with balsamic reduction. For sides and decoration grill one tomato stuffed with sautéed eggplant and caramelized onion. Add a trio of polenta.

FEATURED CHEF

Chef Lipar

TORINO

Executive Chef Garrett Lipar is a 27-year-old culinary genius who has been praised by restaurant critic Christopher Cook for creating a sublime dining heaven at a level rarely seen before around Detroit. Torino earned *Hour Detroit's* Restaurant of the Year in 2015. Lipar grew up in Waterford enjoying the seasons and spending countless hours in his grandparents' vast garden, growing, tasting, canning, and pickling everything he could. At 14 years old, Lipar got a job in a kitchen doing dishes. Before long, he fell in love with the industry and all aspects of it, eventually working his way up to line cook, and soon thereafter heading to Scottsdale Culinary Institute in Arizona. Immediately after finishing school, he received an internship at Public Restaurant in New York City where, under Chef Brad Farmerie, he was exposed to professional cooking and the fundamentals of "balanced cuisine."

He soon worked his way to the top of the NYC flagship restaurant, eventually joining the team at BOKA in Chicago. During his time at both aforementioned restaurants, he "staged" as often as he could in order to absorb as much information as possible, including Alinea in Chicago, which was a big influence on him. However, Lipar credits his move to Scandinavia, and the travel and taste that came with it to be, "the biggest part of our style." He attributes it to his time at Restaurant Frantzen in Stockholm, Sweden. He has run the helm of Torino since February 2013, and lives in Ferndale.

Chef Johns

GRANGE KITCHEN AND BAR

Chef Brandon Johns brings to Grange a passion for fresh, seasonal, and locally sourced menu items. Grange features a regional, evolving menu highlighting the best products and ingredients from local and sustainable sources, prepared simply to accentuate their natural flavors.

Johns began in Ann Arbor behind the line at Real Seafood Company. Shortly after, he moved to New York City and attended the Institute of Culinary Education.

Formally trained in New York City, Johns has cooked in kitchens in New York and Chicago. Since returning to Ann Arbor, Johns has led kitchens at several local establishments, including the Chop House in Ann Arbor.

Johns' love of food began at the age of 5 when his family moved to a property that had once been a farm. His earliest food memories include sitting in a cherry tree eating ripe sour cherries, the smell of ripe Concord grapes, and picking an endless supply of green beans from the family garden. He credits this early introduction to food as the beginning of his passion for using local foods.

At Grange, 80 percent of ingredients are sourced from within 100 miles of the restaurant. Johns has developed an extensive network of local farmers and purveyors, and is an expert in local food sourcing.

He is also known for using the whole animal, and has an affinity for unusual cuts and interesting combinations. His menus feature housemade sausages, unique whole animal dishes like his signature fried pig's head, and changing selections of housemade charcuterie.

Johns is a member of many local food initiatives, and is an honorary chef for the March of Dimes Signature Chef's Auction. He's also been honored as best chef/restaurant in the 2008 and 2011 *Edible WOW* Local Heroes Awards.

Johns lives in Ypsilanti with his wife, Sara, and two daughters, Lily and Alice.

Charred Octopus

with Pickled Watermelon & Green Tomato Gazpacho

CHEF HALBERG | SERVES: 4-6

Octopus Ingredients:

2 pounds frozen octopus, thawed and rinsed

3 garlic cloves, finely chopped

1 celery rib, halved lengthwise and thinly sliced crosswise

1 carrot, halved lengthwise and very thinly sliced crosswise

1/4 cup extra-virgin olive oil

1/4 cup fresh lemon juice

1/2 teaspoon fine sea salt

1/4 teaspoon dried oregano

1/3 cup flat-leaf parsley, chopped

Pickled Watermelon Ingredients:

1 quart seedless watermelon rind, cut into 1-inch square pieces

1/2 cup water

1 cup vinegar, rice wine or plain white vinegar

1 cup sugar

2 1/2 teaspoons table salt or 3 3/4 teaspoons kosher salt

1 star anise

1 2-inch piece peeled ginger, roughly chopped, or 1/2 teaspoon powdered cinnamon

Directions:

1| Cut off and discard head of octopus, and cut tentacles into 1 inch pieces.

2| Generously cover octopus with water in a heavy medium pot and gently simmer, uncovered, until tender, about 45 minutes to 1 hour.

3| Drain octopus in a colander and cool to room temperature. Sear the octopus on a hot grill for about 3-4 minutes until golden brown.

4| Chop tentacles into 1/2-inch pieces, then transfer to a bowl. Stir in remaining ingredients (except parsley), and additional sea salt to taste.

5| Let stand 30 minutes for flavors to develop. Stir in parsley just before serving.

6| For the pickled watermelon, scoop out flesh from half a watermelon, reserving for another use. Leave about 1/2-inch of red flesh on the rind (optional, but colorful and tasty). Cut rind into 1-inch strips, and using a vegetable peeler or knife, remove the bright green watermelon skin from the rind.

7| Combine vinegar, water, sugar, salt, star anise, and ginger in a saucepan with the watermelon rind. Bring to a boil, stirring to dissolve the sugar and salt.

8| When it reaches a boil, add the watermelon rind. Return to boil. Simmer for 1 minute.

9| Remove pan from heat. Cool for 1 hour.

10| Transfer watermelon rind to a 1-quart plastic container, or canning jar. Add as much of the vinegar mixture as will fit in the jar. Refrigerate.

11| Eat the watermelon rind in 1-2 hours, but it tastes better after it's thoroughly chilled (overnight works best).

Green Tomato Gazpacho
Ingredients:

2 1/4 pounds green tomatoes, Coarsely chopped

1 1 pound English hothouse cucumber, coarsely chopped

1/4 cup shallot, chopped

1/2 jalapeño, seeded and chopped

1 teaspoon fresh cilantro, minced

1 garlic clove, minced

1 tablespoon honey

1 1/2 inch-thick slice white country bread, cut into pieces

1/2 cup extra-virgin olive oil

1/3 cup fresh lime juice

1 1/2 tablespoons finely grated lime zest

1 tablespoon fresh basil, minced

Kosher salt and freshly ground black pepper

1 cup green melon

1 tablespoon fresh mint leaves, thinly sliced

Directions:

1| Place first 6 ingredients in a blender. Purée until smooth.

2| With machine running, gradually add honey, then bread, then oil. Purée until smooth.

3| Transfer to a large bowl.

4| Stir in juice, zest, and basil. Season with salt and pepper. Cover. Chill until cold. Garnish soup with melon and mint.

Lamb Chops
with Fried Artichokes & Fava Bean Salad
CHEF HOLLYDAY | SERVES: 6

Lamb
Ingredients:

12 lamb chops

1/2 cup olive oil

4 cloves garlic, minced

1 tablespoon rosemary, chopped

1 tablespoon oregano, chopped

1 pinch of chili flakes

Zest of 1 lemon

Directions:

1| Marinate lamb chops with oil, garlic, rosemary, oregano, chili flakes, and zest for 2 hours or up to overnight.

2| Remove chops from marinade, and discard the marinade. Season with salt and pepper.

3| Heat a grill to medium/medium-high heat. Cook to preferred doneness.

Artichokes
Ingredients:

6 baby artichokes, cleaned and quartered

2 cups olive oil for frying

1/2 cup all-purpose flour

Salt and pepper, to taste

Directions:

1| Set up steamer basket and place artichokes inside. Steam 2-3 minutes or until tender. Allow to cool.

2| When ready to fry, heat olive oil in a medium sauté pan on medium heat. Toss artichokes in flour. Place one artichoke piece to test if oil is hot enough. It should immediately start to sizzle. Add remaining artichoke pieces. Do in small batches to not crowd the pan. Fry until sides are golden brown.

3| Remove and set on plate lined with paper towels to absorb excess oil. Season lightly with salt and pepper. Set aside.

Fava Bean Salad
Ingredients:

2 cups fava beans, blanched and shucked

1 shallot, minced

Juice of 1 lemon

1 tablespoon Calabrian chili, minced

1/2 cup olive oil

2 tablespoons parsley, chopped

Salt and pepper, to taste

Directions:

1| Dress fava beans with shallot, lemon, chili, olive oil, and parsley. Season to taste. Set aside.

Assembly of Dish:

Place two grilled lamb chops per plate. Evenly distribute fava bean salad on and around chops. Place fried artichokes on top and around the plate.

Cold Duck Three Ways
with Strawberry Jelly, Duck Ham & Duck Terrine

CHEF GROSZ | SERVES: 4-6

Torchon with Strawberry Jelly
Ingredients:

1 pound foie gras

2 ounces cognac

1 teaspoon salt

1 teaspoon white pepper

4 cups chicken stock

Directions:

1| Let foie gras sit at room temperature for 1 hour. Devein.

2| Marinate with cognac, salt, and pepper for 10 minutes at room temperature. Wrap in cheesecloth or plastic wrap into a round cylinder shape.

3| Poach in chicken stock for 10 minutes. Wrap tightly in plastic wrap and refrigerate. Once cooled, slice.

Strawberry Jelly
Ingredients:

1 cup strawberry purée

4 gelatin leaves

Directions:

1| Bloom gelatin into strawberry purée. Chill.

Duck Ham
Ingredients:

4 duck breasts

The Brine:

1 cup water

1/2 teaspoon pink salt

1 tablespoon salt

1 teaspoon sugar

1 ounce Madeira or sherry wine

Directions:

1| Add brine ingredients in a pot and bring to a boil. Chill.

2| Brine duck breasts for 8 hours.

3| Hot smoke duck breasts at 180° or bake at 350° until internal temperature reaches 155°. Chill.

Duck Terrine

Ingredients:

1 whole duck

6 ounces pork fat

10 ounces pork shoulder meat

1/2 teaspoon pink curing salt

1 shallot

1 teaspoon garlic

2 ounces cognac

1 ounce Madeira wine

1 duck liver

2 eggs

1 cup white bread, diced

1 teaspoon dried thyme

1 teaspoon garam masala, optional

Garnish:

1/2 cup ham, diced

1/2 cup dried cherries, chopped

Balsamic glaze, your pick

Directions:

1| Debone duck. Trim all fat off the meat.

2| Dice duck, pork fat, and shoulder meat into 1 inch pieces.

3| Mix all ingredients except garnish. Chill.

4| Grind with medium die. Chill.

5| Fold in garnish. Chill.

6| Line terrine mold with plastic wrap overlapping to cover top. Fill with mixture.

7| Bake in water bath at 325° until internal temperature reaches 155°. Cool. Serve with balsamic glaze.

Roasted Skuna Bay Salmon

Chestnut Mousse, Pickled Mustard Seeds, Creamed Kale & Horseradish-Ham Bone Broth

CHEF RIGATO | SERVES: 16-20

Ingredients:

1 whole Skuna Bay salmon fillet (8 lbs.)

10% salt solution

1/4 cup fennel seed

1/4 cup peppercorn, roughly ground

2 tablespoons of coriander, toasted and coarsely ground

Sliced oranges, onions, thyme, and sage, to taste

Directions:

1| Remove the pin bones and skin of the salmon. Brine in salt solution for 20 minutes.

2| Roast salmon on sheet tray generously covered in sliced onions, oranges, thyme, sage, and coriander. Just before roasting add the fennel seed and peppercorn.

3| Roast at 250° for 15 minutes on low fan until medium-rare. When in doubt, turn the temperature down.

Chestnut Mousse

Ingredients:

2 pounds chestnuts, cleaned

5 cups chicken stock

Fresh thyme

1/4 cup Pedro Ximénez Cherry

Directions:

1| Simmer the nuts in the chicken stock with fresh thyme.

2| Purée the chestnuts with Pedro Ximénez Cherry in a Vitamix until smooth.

Pickled Mustard Seeds

Chef Rigato suggests David Chang's mustard seeds from the *Momofuku* cookbook.

Creamed Kale

Ingredients:

>1 large Spanish onion, diced small
>1/4 cup butter
>8 cups local Sunseed Farms kale, cleaned, chopped
>1 quart cream
>1 cup white wine
>½ cup pecorino
>1 lemon
>Salt and pepper, to taste
>Tabasco, to taste

Directions:

1| Sweat the onion in a sauté pan with butter. Then add the kale, and cream and cook until it softens. Season, to taste.

2| After mixing all ingredients together, spoon creamed kale in bowl and set aside until ready to assemble dish.

Horseradish-Ham Bone Broth

Ingredients:

>3 ham bones
>2 gallons of very rich chicken stock
>2 cups horseradish
>Xanthan gum, to taste

Directions:

1| Simmer the ham bones together for 2 hours on low heat in the chicken stock.

2| Strain once time is up and add the horseradish.

3| Blend with xanthan gum until thickened to your desired texture. Start with a teaspoon.

4| Strain through cheesecloth.

Assembly of Dish:

Tear large pieces of salmon and place on top of creamed kale. Garnish with mustard seed. Gently pour broth in bowl up to level of salmon.

Grilled Baby Octopus

Warm Sunseed Farms Potato Salad, Favas, Olives & Romesco Sauce

CHEF RIGATO | SERVES: 4-6

Grilled Octopus

Ingredients:

>2 pounds baby octopi, cleaned and rinsed
>Court bouillon, see below
>Olive oil, as needed

Directions:

1| Poach the baby octopi in the court bouillon. Simmer for 30-40 minutes.

2| Split into halves once cooked with a sharp knife.

3| Dress in olive oil. Sear the octopus on a hot grill for about 3-4 minutes until golden brown.

Court Bouillon

Ingredients:

>1 bottle dry white wine
>3 cups water
>Salt, to taste
>1 lemon, sliced and squeezed
>1 onion, roughly chopped
>4 tablespoons pickling spice

Directions:

1| Combine all ingredients to be used for poaching the octopi.

Potato Salad

Ingredients:

> 4 pounds heirloom potatoes, diced into medium/large cubes
>
> 2 stalks celery, small diced
>
> 2 tablespoons chives
>
> 1/2 cup Spanish olive oil, more if necessary
>
> 1/2 cup Champagne vinegar
>
> Salt, to taste
>
> Tabasco, to taste
>
> 20 pods of fava beans, shucked, peeled, blanched in salt water
>
> 1 cup Picholine olives, pitted, lightly roasted

Directions:

1| Simmer the potatoes in salted water until just tender. Drain.

2| Mix with all the other ingredients, reserving the olives for the very end. Keep warm and serve soon after mixing.

Romesco

Ingredients:

> 1 large onion, roughly chopped
>
> Olive oil, as needed
>
> 6 cloves garlic, smashed
>
> 1 large tomato, diced
>
> 3 dried pasilla chiles, crumbled
>
> 2 tablespoons smoked paprika
>
> 1 cup slivered almonds
>
> 1 cup dry Spanish white wine
>
> 3/4 cup red wine vinegar
>
> Salt, to taste

Directions:

1| Sauté the onion in olive oil until soft. Add garlic until toasty. Add chiles, tomatoes, and almond. Sauté another minute or so.

2| Add paprika and white wine. Cook until white wine is dissolved. Add red wine vinegar.

3| Purée in a blender or food processor until very smooth. Season with salt.

Soba Gnocchi

with Scallops & Celery Root Foam

CHEF YAGIHASHI | SERVES: 4

Gnocchi

Ingredients:

> 1 large Idaho potato
>
> 2 tablespoons Parmesan cheese, grated
>
> 1/2 teaspoon extra-virgin olive oil
>
> 1/2 lightly beaten egg
>
> 1/2 teaspoon kosher salt and pepper
>
> 1/4 cup all-purpose flour, plus more for dusting
>
> 1/4 cup buckwheat flour
>
> 2 tablespoons vegetable oil

Directions:

1| Preheat the oven to 400°.

2| Using a fork, poke several small holes into the potato. Place it onto a baking sheet. Bake the potato for 1 1/2 hours, or until the potato is soft to the touch.

3| Split the potato in half while still hot. Use a spoon to scoop out the inside, discarding the skin.

4| Grind the potato through a food mill or ricer, and combine it with Parmesan cheese, olive oil, egg, salt, and pepper.

5| Add both flours until you have a smooth, creamy texture, not overworking the dough.

6| Dust a work surface with all-purpose flour and divide the dough into four portions.

7| Gently roll one portion of the dough on the counter to create a long rope, a 1/2 inch thick. Cover the remaining dough with a dry towel.

8| Lightly pinch the rolled dough between your thumb and index finger.

9| Use a paring knife to cut the dough into 1-inch long pieces. Each piece should resemble a small pillow. Repeat until all dough is used.

10| Prepare an ice bath and bring a large pot of heavily salted water to a boil. Add 1/4 of the gnocchi and cook until the gnocchi have risen to the surface, 1-2 minutes.

11| Remove the gnocchi from the water and submerge in the ice bath. Drain to cool follow the same process to cook the rest of the gnocchi.

12| Once cooked, lightly toss gnocchi in vegetable oil.

Celery Root Foam
Ingredients:
- 1 tablespoon extra-virgin olive oil
- 1/2 white portion of 1 leek, rinsed well, thinly sliced
- 1/2 onion, thinly sliced
- 1 tablespoon minced garlic
- 2 1/4 teaspoons salt
- 1 1/2 cups celery root cubed
- 4 cups water
- 3/4 cup half-and-half
- 1 cup skim milk
- 1 tablespoon unsalted butter
- White pepper

Directions:
1| Place a saucepan over medium heat. After 30 seconds, add the olive oil and let it heat for one minute. It should be hot, but not smoking.

2| Add the leek, onion, garlic, and 1/4 tablespoon of salt. Decrease the heat to low and cook. Stirring often, until the vegetables are translucent, about 5 minutes.

3| Add the celery root and cook for 2 minutes longer. Add the water and bring just to a boil before decreasing the heat to medium-low.

4| Simmer until the celery root becomes soft, about 30 minutes.

5| Remove the saucepan from the heat and let it sit at room temperature, until mostly cool, about 15 minutes.

6| To finish the foam, combine the half-and-half, skim milk, butter, and remaining 1 1/2 teaspoons salt, and white pepper in a blender.

7| Add the cooled celery root mixture and blend on high speed until smooth. Strain the sauce through a fine mesh sieve into a pot.

8| Heat over low heat until the liquid begins to simmer, then turn off the heat and cover.

Assembly of Dish:
- 1/4 cup extra-virgin olive oil
- 2 royal trumpet mushrooms, cut into quarters lengthwise, then 2-inch long pieces
- 1/2 teaspoon kosher salt
- 1 tablespoon unsalted butter
- Gnocchi
- 1 tablespoon minced shallot
- Garlic clove, minced
- 1/2 cup heavy cream
- 2 tablespoons Parmesan cheese, grated
- 1 tablespoon parsley, minced
- 16 large scallops
- 2 tablespoons olive oil
- Pinch of salt and white pepper

Cook the mushrooms in 2 tablespoons of olive oil, with salt, for about 4 minutes until browned.

Add butter. Once melted, add shallots, garlic, and gnocchi. Cook until gnocchi are browned, then decrease heat to low. Add heavy cream and cheese to thicken sauce. Add parsley.

Cook scallops in separate saucepan in 2 tablespoons of olive oil with salt and pepper, about 2 minutes, until the bottoms have browned. Turn over, and reduce heat to low. Cook for an additional 2 minutes.

Lastly, heat the foam mixture to a simmer, and transfer it to a tall, narrow container. Use an immersion blender to "foam" the sauce and create bubbles. To serve, divide the gnocchi and sauce among 4 shallow bowls. Top each with 4 scallops and foam.

Chef Polcyn

FOREST GRILL

Chef Brian Polcyn is an award-winning chef and charcuterie expert. Nationally recognized for his creativity and culinary talents, he's known as the visionary behind some of Detroit's most acclaimed restaurants.

While still in his 20s, Polcyn honed his skills at two of Michigan's most prestigious restaurants, The Golden Mushroom and The Lark.

In 1990, he premiered Chimayo, Michigan's first restaurant featuring authentic Southwestern cuisine. Three years later, he created Acadia, an area trendsetter specializing in foods cooked over various hardwoods. And in Milford, Polcyn opened Five Lakes Grill and Cinco Lagos. In 2008, he opened the Forest Grill in Birmingham.

The Forest Grill is an American bistro that provides fine food by incorporating elements of traditional European cooking techniques, modern American cuisine, and exceptional ingredients.

Polcyn was prominently featured as the expert in Michael Ruhlman's popular book, *The Soul of a Chef: The Journey Toward Perfection*. And in 2005, they teamed up again to publish *Charcuterie: The Craft of Salting, Smoking, and Curing*, which was a 2006 James Beard Award nominee.

In 2012, Polcyn and Ruhlman published the follow-up book to *Charcuterie*, called *Salumi: The Craft of Italian Dry Curing*. Polcyn also teaches about charcuterie on the road with Cuisine University. He is also a faculty member at Schoolcraft College, and does consulting at Garden Fresh in Ferndale.

With numerous awards under his belt, some highlights include three gold medals and a silver medal from The American Culinary Federation, and a nomination for Best Chef in the Midwest in 2006 by the James Beard Foundation. He's cooked several times at the James Beard House in New York City, and participates at the Traverse City Epicurean Classic and StarChefs International Chefs Congress. He is also involved with many local charities.

Chef Polisei

OCEAN PRIME

Chef Adam Polisei began his restaurant career at Harper's Restaurant and Brew Pub in East Lansing, while completing a degree in food industry management from Michigan State University. He then ventured to Mitchell's Fish Market in 2006, where he was quickly promoted from broil cook to sous chef of the restaurant's Cincinnati location. From there, Polisei relocated to Florida, where he was sous chef of Ocean Prime in Tampa.

The Clinton Township native was captivated with the restaurant business from a young age and proved that his enthusiasm in the kitchen was contagious. Shadowing his uncle at Hungry Howie's, Polisei eagerly completed any task he was allowed to as a 10-year-old. Once he realized the joy he could bring to people by creating in the kitchen, he was hooked.

As a child, Polisei idolized his grandfather, a hospitality industry veteran, who regaled him with stories of Polisei's great-grandfather immigrating to the United States and making a living as a chef at the Detroit Hotel. Knowing how proud his great-grandfather would be of his culinary accomplishments has been a great inspiration for Polisei throughout his career.

When not experimenting in the kitchen, Polisei and his wife, Heather, love enjoying food and wine together, cheering on the Detroit Tigers, and soaking up the outdoors while fishing and golfing.

Pan Seared Duck Breast

with Wilted Kale, Roasted Chanterelles, Quinoa Cake & Butternut Squash Purée

CHEF CONSTANTINE | SERVES: 4

Duck Breast Ingredients:

4 boneless duck breasts

Kosher salt and freshly ground black pepper, to taste

Wilted Kale Ingredients:

2 large bunches kale, Swiss chard, or mustard greens, rinsed

1/4 cup olive oil

1 medium yellow onion, thinly sliced

1 cup grape tomatoes, cut in half

2 tablespoons red wine vinegar

1 1/2 teaspoons kosher salt

Directions:

1| Preheat the oven to 400°.

2| Score the skin of the duck breast with a knife in 2 directions, crossing over each other (make a crosshatch). Do not cut into the meat, just the skin. Season both sides of each duck breast with salt and pepper.

3| In a large nonstick skillet over low heat, place the duck breasts skin side down. Sear the breasts until the skin is golden brown; this will take a while. You must render all the fat under the skin to ensure crispy duck skin; about 20 minutes.

4| Flip and sear the other side for 3 minutes. Place the seared duck breasts in a baking dish skin side up, and put them in oven. Bake for 5-6 minutes depending on size. You want to serve your duck breast at 125°. Remove the duck breasts from the oven and allow them to rest for 5 minutes.

Wilted Kale
Directions:
1| Tear the kale greens into pieces; discard stems.

2| In a sauté pan, over medium heat, heat the oil. Add the onion and cook for 7 minutes. Add the greens and toss to coat, add tomatoes and red wine vinegar. Cover and cook, stirring once, until wilted, about 2 minutes. Add the salt and serve.

Quinoa Cake
Ingredients:
> 2 1/2 cups cooked hot quinoa
> 1 teaspoon salt
> 1/4 teaspoon freshly ground pepper
> 2 tablespoons chopped parsley
> 1/2 small onion, finely chopped (1/3 cup)
> 1 cup fresh Parmesan cheese, grated
> 3/4 cup heavy cream
>
> Three-Step Breading
> 1 cup flour
> 4 large eggs, whisked
> 1 cup panko breadcrumbs
> 2 tablespoon oil, more as needed

Directions:
1| Combine the quinoa, salt, pepper, onion, parsley, Parmesan cheese, and heavy cream in a large bowl. Mix to combine.

2| Spread mixture on cookie sheet lined with parchment paper. Place in fridge to firm up.

3| When quinoa cake mixture is cold, turn out on a cutting board and cut it in to squares.

4| In three separate bowls, place flour, whisked eggs, and breadcrumbs in their own bowl.

5| Take each cold quinoa square and first dip it in flour, then into the egg, and lastly into the breadcrumbs. Place on a cookie sheet and finish the remaining quinoa squares.

6| Heat the oil in a large skillet over medium-low heat, add 5-6 patties, cover, and cook for 3 minutes until the bottoms are deeply browned. Carefully flip the patties with a spatula and cook the other sides for 3 minutes, or until golden.

7| Remove from the skillet and cool on a large plate. Add more oil to the skillet if needed between each batch.

Butternut Squash Purée
Ingredients:
> 2 butternut squash (about 1 pound each)
> 4 tablespoons softened butter, divided
> Salt and pepper, to taste

Directions:
1| Halve the squash lengthwise and remove the seeds and strings. Rub the insides with 2 tablespoons softened butter; season with salt and pepper. Place on a roasting pan, skin side down.

2| Bake in a preheated 350° oven for 30-40 minutes or until fork tender. Remove the squash from the oven, scoop out the flesh and place in a food processor.

3| Add remaining 2 tablespoons of butter. Purée until smooth. Add a pinch of salt. Pulse a few times to incorporate.

Roasted Chanterelle Sauce
Ingredients:
> 1/4 cup unsalted butter
> 1 pound fresh chanterelle mushrooms, sliced (if small enough, you can leave them whole)
> 1 medium onion, chopped
> 1/3 cup whipping cream
> 1/3 cup brandy
> 1 cup veal stock
> Salt and pepper, to taste
> Chopped fresh parsley

Directions:
1| Melt the unsalted butter in a large heavy skillet over medium high heat. Add the mushrooms and the onion to the skillet. Sauté over medium-high heat until the mushrooms begin to brown and almost all of the liquid has reduced. This should take roughly 12 minutes.

2| Add the cream and brandy to the mushrooms. Pour in the veal stock. Simmer this mixture until thickened almost to a sauce consistency, about 8 minutes. Season to taste with salt and pepper and sprinkle with parsley.

Tortellaccio

Big Tortellino Stuffed with Braised Beef,
Cream of Porcini Mushroom & Leeks

CHEF DELL' ACQUA | SERVES: 8

Sfoglia (Egg Noodle Dough)
Ingredients:

- 4 cups flour
- 1 1/2 cup eggs
- 1/4 cup water
- 1 tablespoon olive oil

Directions:

1| Put flour in large bowl. Pour eggs, water, and oil in center. Mix and knead.

2| Roll flat or use a pasta machine to make long 3-inch wide strips of thin dough. Cut into 4-inch squares, and put a ball of filling in each (see below).

3| Bring opposite corners together like a triangle making sure you brush the side of the square with beaten eggs. Pinch and seal filling inside, and twist lower corners together. Boil 15-20 minutes.

Filling
Ingredients:

- 1 carrot
- 1 celery head
- 1 onion
- 1 leek
- 1 teaspoon salt
- 2 teaspoons ground black pepper
- Chicken stock, as needed
- 3 fresh porcini mushrooms, cooked
- 1 pound of ground veal, tender, seasoned, and pan seared to medium
- 1 1/8 cup ricotta cheese
- 3 eggs
- 1 cup freshly grated Parmesan cheese
- 1 cup of fresh Italian parsley, chopped
- 2 teaspoons nutmeg
- Extra-virgin olive oil, to cook

Directions:

1| Wash and cut all the vegetables. Cook them with extra-virgin olive oil for 10 minutes.

2| Add the meat, salt, and pepper. Cook the ground meat for 1 hour making sure to add a little chicken stock, as needed.

3| When ready add porcini mushrooms that have already been cooked separately.

4| Chill and blend everything else in a bowl. Mix and form into 3/4-inch size balls for the filling.

For the Sauce
Ingredients:

- 4 pieces fresh leek
- 2 scallions
- 1 teaspoon garlic, minced
- White wine, as needed
- 1 cup of peas
- 1 tablespoon extra-virgin olive oil
- 1/4 stick of butter
- 2 cups heavy whipping cream
- Salt and pepper, to taste

Directions:

1| Cut leeks and scallions. Sauté in oil until golden brown.

2| Add garlic, and add white wine until it evaporates. Add the peas, salt, and pepper.

3| Add butter and the whipping cream until reduced. While still hot, finish it in a blender for smooth consistency.

4| Reheat the sauce for 5 minutes and top your tortellaccio with the sauce. Add fried and crispy sliced leeks for a tasteful decoration.

Local Rabbit Confit

with Ricotta Gnocchi, Spring Peas, Garlic, Ramps, Morels & Rabbit Broth

CHEF RIGATO | SERVES: 8-12

Rabbit Confit
Ingredients:

2 fresh rabbits, broken down into primal cuts, cured for 12 hours

Olive oil, duck fat, or pork fat, enough to submerge rabbit

Rabbit Cure
Ingredients:

1 cup kosher salt

1 cup brown sugar

1 bunch thyme

2 oranges, zested

1 tablespoon roughly cracked peppercorn, toasted

3 tablespoons torn sage leaves

Directions:

1| Season the rabbit heavily with the entire cure. Lay flat. Refrigerate. After 12 hours, rinse thoroughly and pat dry.

2| Let air dry in the refrigerator for another 12 hours if you have time.

3| Submerge the rabbit in fat (olive oil, duck fat, or pork fat) and cook in the oven at 250°-275° for 4-6 hours.

4| Check the rabbit at 4 hours for tenderness. When tender and the meat slips easily away from the bone, remove from oven.

5| Let cool in the fat until the meat can easily be handled. When meat is cool enough, pull the meat from the bone and save the bones. Once all the meat is saved, set aside.

6| Strain the fat. Cool. Once the fat is cooled there should be a layer of liquid at the bottom. This is called the "gold." Dig for the gold and set aside.

7| The fat can be reused for another confit, frozen, and used to fry other foods in.

Rabbit Broth
Ingredients:

1 gallon rich chicken stock

Rabbit bones from the confit

Rabbit gold

2 carrots, peeled, chopped

2 parsnips, peeled, chopped

1 large onion, peeled, chopped

3 stalks celery, cleaned chopped

4 cloves garlic

Directions:

1| Combine all ingredients in a stock pot, and simmer. Simmer this broth for about 2-4 hours, depending on the richness of the original stock. Strain. Taste. May need salt and a squeeze of lemon.

Roasted Garlic
Ingredients:

2 whole bulbs of garlic

Directions:

1| Cut garlic bulbs across the top. Drizzle with olive oil. Wrap in foil. Roast in the oven for about 1 hour. Squeeze bulbs out of garlic. Set aside.

Spring Peas
Ingredients:

1/2 pound fresh spring peas in the shell, shucked and blanched or use 1 cup frozen peas

Ramps
Ingredients:

20 fresh ramps

Directions:
1| Cut the ramps where the stalk turns green and becomes the leaves. Rough chop the leaves.

2| Slice the stems across into tiny "coins". Pickle them. (see below)

Pickling Liquid
Ingredients:
- 1 cup apple cider vinegar
- 1 tablespoon salt
- 1 tablespoon sugar
- 1 lemon juice
- 1 teaspoon turmeric
- 1 teaspoon dried mustard powder

Directions:
1| Boil this liquid. Pour over the ramp stems.

Morels
Ingredients:
- 1 pound morels, split in half
- Butter

Ricotta Filling
Ingredients:
- Ricotta
- 1 gallon milk
- 1 cup cream
- Salt, to taste
- 4 cups buttermilk
- Splash of lemon

Directions:
1| Heat milk, cream, and salt slowly until it begins to separate into curds and whey.

2| Add lemon juice and gently stir. Milk will curdle. Let sit a few minutes. Gently strain through cheesecloth.

3| Depending on the fat content of the milk you will have a different quantity of ricotta. Measure what your finished ricotta is.

Gnocchi
Ingredients:
- 1 cup ricotta
- Zest of 1 lemon
- 1 cup flour
- 1/2 cup pecorino
- 1 egg

Directions:
1| Mix everything except flour in a bowl.

2| Add flour slowly and gently. Pipe dough out of pastry bag. Gently roll with more flour.

3| Cut. Place on a tray. Freeze or chill before using.

Assembly of Dish:
Boil the gnocchi until they float for approximately 2-4 minutes.

Meanwhile in a large, hot sauté pan, sauté the morels in butter. Once cooked add the ramps, greens, peas, and pulled rabbit meat, and a splash of the rabbit broth. Pull the gnocchi out of the water and right into the pan. Season with grated pecorino. Spoon gently into a bowl. Add rabbit broth to desired quantity, about half way up the side of the sauté pan. Top with shaved pecorino and a drizzle of the confit oil. Serve.

Escabeche of Michigan Shrimp

with Tomato Fennel Relish &
Parsley Coulis

CHEF GREEN | SERVES: 4-6

Shrimp Escabeche

Ingredients:

> 1 red onion, cut in half and sliced thin crosswise
>
> 1/2 cup white vinegar
>
> 1/4 teaspoon fresh oregano
>
> 1 teaspoon salt
>
> 2/3 cup olive oil
>
> 2 bay leaves
>
> 2 garlic cloves, smashed
>
> 1 teaspoon black peppercorns
>
> 2 pounds shrimp

Directions:

1| In a non-reactive dish combine onion, vinegar, oregano, and salt.

2| In a stainless steel pan simmer the olive oil, bay leaves, garlic, and peppercorns for 10 minutes. Remove from heat and allow to cool.

3| Add the shrimp to a pot of boiling salted water. Remove from heat and allow to sit uncovered for 5 minutes.

4| Mix the oil and onion mixtures. Drain the shrimp, and add to the combined mixture.

5| Allow the shrimp to chill in the escabeche, stirring occasionally for at least 12 hours.

6| Discard the bay leaves. Serve the shrimp cold or at room temperature.

Parsley Coulis

Ingredients:

> 10 parsley leaves, no stems
>
> 1/4 teaspoon kosher salt
>
> 1/4 teaspoon vitamin C powder
>
> 1/2 cup crushed ice

Directions:

1| Shock the parsley in a pot of boiling water for 10 seconds. Then quickly shock the parsley in a bowl with ice and water.

2| Wring the parsley out in a linen napkin.

3| In a Vitamix purée the parsley, salt, vitamin C powder, and a little of the ice to keep it from getting warm.

4| Repeat until the ice is gone and coulis is a vibrant green with a smooth consistency.

Tomato Fennel Relish

Ingredients:

> 2/3 cup Roma tomato, seeded and diced
>
> 1/3 cup fennel, finely diced
>
> 1 tablespoon fresh orange juice
>
> 1/2 teaspoon orange peel
>
> 2 teaspoons olive oil
>
> 1/4 teaspoon kosher salt
>
> 2 garlic cloves, minced

Directions:

1| In a stainless steel bowl combine the tomatoes, fennel, orange juice, orange peel, olive oil, salt, and garlic together.

2| Allow this mixture to sit overnight.

Lamb Merguez

with Carrot Purée &
Candied Grapefruit Peel

CHEF GILBERT | YIELD: 4 LBS. SAUSAGE

Merguez Sausage
Ingredients:

3 pounds cleaned lamb shoulder, cubed

1 pound pork fat, cubed

Lamb casings, cleaned

Spice Blend:

2 teaspoons whole cumin

2 teaspoons whole coriander

2 teaspoons whole black pepper

2 teaspoons whole fennel

3 tablespoons freshly chopped garlic

3 tablespoons chopped parsley

3 tablespoons paprika

3 tablespoons kosher salt

1 teaspoon cayenne pepper

Directions:

1| Chill grinder attachments and pan for ground meat.

2| Toast whole spices in hot pan until bloomed. Grind and combine with garlic, parsley, paprika, salt and cayenne.

3| Toss cubed meat and fat with spices. Chill.

4| Grind meat through small die into chilled pan, ideally in an ice bath.

5| Mix on low speed for 1 minute with paddle attachment until meat and fat are fully incorporated and sausage is sticky. Cook tester sausage and adjust seasoning.

6| Stuff sausage into lamb casings. Twist into desired link length.

7| Cook sausage on grill or in a pan to the proper tempurature.

Carrot Purée
Ingredients:

5 large carrots

2:1 simple syrup (2 parts sugar, 1 part water)

1 tablespoon butter

Salt and pepper, to taste

Directions:

1| Peel carrots. Cover with simple syrup and cook until fork tender.

2| Purée in Vita-Prep until smooth, using cooking liquid to thin out if necessary.

3| Add the butter at the end for added creaminess. Season with salt and pepper.

Candied Grapefruit
Ingredients:

4 grapefruit

1 quart red beet juice

Directions:

1| Peel grapefruit. Remove all pith from zest.

2| Cover grapefruit skin with cold water and bring to a boil. After water has reached a boil, strain hot liquid, cover with cold water, and bring to a boil again. Repeat this 3 times.

3| On fourth boil, strain water and add enough beet juice to cover skins. Poach over low heat for 45 minutes.

4| Remove from heat and cool in poaching liquid.

Chef Rigato

THE ROOT RESTAURANT & BAR

James Rigato is the executive chef of The Root Restaurant & Bar in White Lake where he features Midwestern flavors and a commitment to sustainable sourcing. The Howell native and Schoolcraft College graduate finds his cooking philosophy stems from a lifelong love of food and an appreciation for the diverse agricultural area where he was raised. His Italian grandparents were early culinary influences, exposing him to Italian culture and the art of handcrafted cuisine that's shaped his approach to the chef profession.

Rigato entered the restaurant business at age 14 as a dishwasher at a local diner. After enrolling in Schoolcraft College's culinary program at 17, he spent the next eight years working in some of metro Detroit's finer restaurants, including Morels, Shiraz, Rugby Grille at The Townsend Hotel, and Bacco Ristorante. In 2007, Rigato accepted a part-time, personal chef position at Royal Oak Recycling after a friend referred him to Ed Mamou, the vice president of Royal Oak Recycling and Royal Oak Storage. Rigato's passion and enthusiasm in the kitchen quickly gained the attention of Mamou who brought him on full-time. Soon, the two began discussing plans for a new venture, a chef-driven restaurant committed to promoting the bounty around the Michigan area. And at age 26, Rigato opened The Root Restaurant & Bar with Mamou. His pursuit of localizing Michigan's food economy stretches into the community, where he does a lot of volunteer work.

Rigato's contemporary American cuisine with a Michigan focus has garnered regional and national attention, including a *Food & Wine* magazine Great Lakes Region nomination for The People's Best New Chef, and *Detroit Free Press*' 2012 Restaurant of the Year award. In 2013, Rigato earned the title of Best Chef by *Hour Detroit*. He's also been featured on the Cooking Channel's newest series *America's Best Bites* and Bravo's series *Top Chef*.

An avid poet and advocate for all things Michigan, Rigato can be found in some corner of the state exploring, cycling, kayaking, eating, or camping.

Chef Somerville

THE LARK

Chef John Somerville joined The Lark in 1994, and served as sous chef until his ascension to chef de cuisine in 2006. Somerville is repeatedly voted the region's finest chef in *Hour Detroit's* Best of Detroit readers' polls, and has achieved national celebrity-chef status with his appearances on Bravo TV's show *Top Chef*. In 2011, Somerville, a multi-James Beard Award finalist, was a featured chef on the James Beard foundation's Celebrity Chef Tour. Somerville is also a 2014 member of the prestigious Best Chefs America.

Alaskan Halibut

Over an Alaskan King Crab Cake

CHEF WARD | SERVES: 4

Ingredients:

Clarified butter, for cooking

4, 4-ounce Alaskan halibut fillets

4, 2-ounce Alaskan king crab cakes

4 ounces asparagus, cleaned and blanched

4 ounces Hon Shimeji mushrooms

8 ounces orange miso beurre blanc

Directions:

1| Preheat oven to 350°.

2| In a sauté pan heat clarified butter to smoke level and sear one side of the halibut until golden brown. Flip them over in the pan, then place the pan in the oven until they are cooked through about 2/3 of the way. This will take about 6-8 minutes.

3| Remove them from the pan and let rest, as it will continue to cook all the way through.

4| In a hot sauté pan with clarified butter, sear the crab cakes on each side until golden brown. Set aside. Sauté the mushrooms for approximately 30 seconds.

5| For the plating, use a bowl and place 2 ounces of the orange miso buerre blanc on the bottom. Add the crab cake. Heat asparagus and place on the cake, then put the halibut on the next layer. Garnish with the mushrooms and serve.

Crab Cakes (Serves 10)
Ingredients:

8 ounces jumbo lump blue crab

8 ounces backfin blue crab meat

4 ounces peeled king crab meat

1 egg, hard-cooked and minced

1 ounce white onion, minced

2 ounces mayonnaise

2 ounces breadcrumbs

Worcestershire sauce, to taste

Tabasco, to taste

Salt and pepper, to taste

15 cilantro leaves, chopped

1 ounce fresh ginger, minced

1 green onion, sliced

Directions:

1| Start by combining the crabmeat with the onion, egg, mayonnaise, breadcrumbs, and seasonings. Then add the cilantro, ginger, and green onion. Mix thoroughly.

2| Form into 2-ounce patties and serve.

Orange Miso Beurre Blanc
Ingredients:

4 cups orange juice

1/4 cup light miso

2 cups heavy cream

1 cup unsalted butter, cut into cubes

Directions:

1| In a large saucepan, add orange juice and cook on medium-high heat until it is reduced to approximately 3/4. This should take roughly 20 minutes. It should have a syrup consistency. Add miso and whisk until fully incorporated.

2| Add the heavy cream and reduce by half. Turn down the heat to medium-low, add butter cubes, and whisk thoroughly. Do not let the sauce boil.

Stuffed Paccheri

with Fresh Ricotta, Parmigiano-Reggiano,
Spinach, Tomato Purée & Chives

CHEF CASADEI | SERVES: 6-8

Vellutata di Pomodoro Sauce

Ingredients:

1/4 cup extra-virgin olive oil
1 teaspoon red pepper flakes
1 small Vidalia onion, chopped
1 small carrot, chopped
1 celery rib, chopped
28-ounce can San Marzano tomatoes
1/4 cup fresh basil
Salt and pepper, to taste
2 ounces cream

Directions:

1| Heat olive oil in a 2-quart saucepan until simmering. Add pepper flakes, onion, carrot, and celery.

2| Sauté until translucent. Add tomatoes. Bring to a boil and simmer for 1 hour.

3| Remove from heat. Add basil, and season with salt and pepper. Purée using immersion blender until smooth.

4| Pass through a fine mesh strainer. Stir in cream and hold warm over stovetop until needed.

Stuffed Paccheri Ricotta Cheese Filling

Ingredients:

1 pound fresh ricotta
1 cup Parmigiano Reggiano, grated
1 egg, beaten
1 tablespoon fresh chives, chopped
2 tablespoons fresh basil, chopped
Salt and pepper, to taste

Directions:

1| Place ricotta in fine mesh strainer, over a bowl, and leave in refrigerator to drain overnight.

2| Combine all ingredients in mixing bowl with drained ricotta. Whisk until smooth.

Fonduta Parmigiano Reggiano Sauce

Ingredients:

1 ounce butter, unsalted
1 ounce flour
1 cup milk
Pinch nutmeg
1/4 cup Parmigiano Reggiano, grated
Salt and white pepper, to taste

Directions:

1| In small saucepan, melt butter. Add flour and cook stirring constantly over low heat for 5 minutes. Do not brown mixture.

2| Add milk and nutmeg. Whisk well and increase heat to medium.

3| Bring to a boil, stirring frequently until sauce becomes thick.

4| Reduce heat to low, add Parmigiano and puré with immersion blender to remove any lumps. Pass through fine mesh strainer.

5| Season with salt and white pepper. Hold warm over very low heat until needed.

Assembly of Dish:

1 pound paccheri pasta
1 ounce extra-virgin olive oil
Ricotta filling
1/4 pound mozzarella, shredded
Vellutata di pomodoro sauce
Fonduta Parmigiano-Reggiano sauce

Preheat oven to 350°. Boil pasta in salted water according to package instructions. Drain pasta and shock in cold water. Drain again, and toss with olive oil. Using pastry bag, pipe ricotta filling into each paccheri tube. Coat a casserole dish with thin layer of vellutata sauce. Line with one layer of stuffed pasta, and sprinkle mozzarella over the top. Bake in oven until pasta just begins to blister, about 10-15 minutes. Ladle 2 ounces of vellutata sauce on the plate. Place 2-3 tubes of stuffed paccheri over the sauce. Cover with 1 ounce of Parmigiano fonduta.

Breast of Squab

with Garnet Yams & Vanilla Butter

CHEF HALBERG | SERVES: 4

Ingredients:

4 whole squab, legs, wings, necks, and backbone removed and reserved

4 tablespoons unsalted butter

1/4 cup Armagnac

2 cups unsalted chicken stock or low-sodium chicken broth

1 tablespoon sherry vinegar

Salt and coarsely ground black pepper

1 tablespoon extra-virgin olive oil

1 shallot, peeled, trimmed, and thinly sliced

Directions:

1| Preheat oven to 400°, with rack in center position.

2| Chop the back, wing, and neck bones into small pieces.

3| Melt 2 tablespoons of the butter in a large sauté pan over high heat. Add the bones and legs. Cook until golden brown.

4| Deglaze and flambé with the Armagnac. Cook until the liquid has evaporated. Add chicken stock and lower the heat to a simmer. Cook until leg meat is tender, about 20 minutes.

5| Remove the legs from the pan and let cool. Season the sauce with sherry vinegar, salt, and pepper. Reduce the liquid by half. Strain the sauce through a fine mesh sieve and reserve.

6| Season the squab breasts with salt and pepper. In a large ovenproof sauté pan, melt the remaining butter and heat oil. Sear the breasts, skin side down, until golden brown. Flip the breasts over and place the pan in the oven. Roast for 4 minutes.

Remove the pan from the oven. Place the squab on a wire rack to rest for a few minutes. Remove the breast meat from the bones, and cut the breast into thin slices. Set aside and keep warm.

7| Serve with reserved sauce, yams, and desired vegetable.

Garnet Yams & Vanilla Butter
Ingredients:

5 pounds garnet yams, scrubbed

1 1/2 sticks salted butter

1 fresh vanilla bean, scraped

1 cup heavy cream

Salt and pepper, to taste

Directions:

1| Preheat oven to 375°.

2| Roast yams until very soft allow to cool enough to handle.

3| Remove skins and combine with softened (not melted) butter, scraped vanilla, cream, salt and pepper.

4| Mash until smooth.

Crisp
Roast Duck

with Herb Dumplings, Wilted Kale & Blood Orange Gastrique

CHEF SOMERVILLE | SERVES: 4

Ingredients:

1 whole Chinese roasted duck or
1 skin-on whole duck breast cooked briefly in a 350° fryer

Directions:

1| Separate breasts and thighs from body.

2| Crisp breast by placing duck breast on baking tray skin side up. Place under hot broiler until skin begins to crisp up.

3| Slice thinly with an electric knife. Repeat crisping procedure with thighs.

Herb Dumplings

Ingredients:

2 pounds potatoes, peeled, and coarsely chopped
2 eggs
1 1/2-2 cups all-purpose flour
1 tablespoon fresh chives, chopped
1 tablespoon parsley
1 tablespoon rosemary
Sea salt and white pepper, to taste
Butter, as needed

Directions:

1| In a sauce pot cover potatoes with lightly salted water. Simmer until potatoes are done. Pass potatoes through a food mill into a kitchen-aid mixing bowl.

2| Add eggs, flour and herbs. Remove a small ball of dough and roll it into long cylindrical worm-like shape.

3| Cut into 1/2-inch pieces. Boil in lightly salted water until dumplings float.

4| Just before serving, lightly sauté in melted butter in a non-stick Teflon sauté pan until lightly browned. Season lightly with sea salt and pepper.

Blood Orange Gastrique

Ingredients:

5 blood oranges, juiced
1/2 cup honey
Cornstarch water, see below
1/2 cup Cointreau

Directions:

1| In a small sauce pot bring juice and honey to a light boil.

2| Make a slurry by combining equal parts arrowroot starch and water.

3| Thicken orange sauce by adding a small amount of slurry. Add Cointreau.

Assembly of Dish:
Amaranth, optional

Place dumplings in the middle of a plate. Place sliced duck breast and thigh on top of dumplings. Spoon blood orange sauce around dumplings on the plate. Garnish with amaranth.

Chef Dell'Acqua

THE SILVER SPOON

Chef Daniele Dell'Acqua is executive chef at The Silver Spoon in Rochester Hills. The restaurant epitomizes the quintessential Italian restaurant adorned with traditional Italian flavor. Dell'Acqua's menu depicts Northern Italian cuisine with an emphasis on fresh ingredients, flavorful fresh and dry pasta, and fresh fish deboned tableside.

Before coming to The Silver Spoon, Chef Dell'Acqua opened and was executive chef at Il Posto Ristorante in Southfield, an *Hour Detroit* Restaurant of the Year in 2006. Il Posto earned and maintained a five-star diamond rating, and Chef Dell'Acqua's menu was used exclusively for events like the Detroit Auto Show and Ryder Cup. After the upscale restaurant closed, he opened Tom's Oyster Bar in Rochester Hills, where he was the executive chef. Dell'Acqua built his culinary reputation in Italy. From 1993-1997, he was executive chef at Moon Fish in Milan, a restaurant that earned four coveted Michelin stars. In 1987, he opened Osteria 101 in Milan where he was chef de cuisine. The restaurant was lauded with three Michelin stars. And in 1999, Dell'Acqua won first prize in the Il Chicco D'oro competition for best risotto.

Variations of Chocolate & Beet,
Recipe on page 133.

Desserts

Red Wine Poached Peach

with Orange Mascarpone

CHEF POLISEI | SERVES: 4

Ingredients:

4 halves of peaches, poached
Red wine reduction
Orange mascarpone
Pistachio shortbread crumbs
Pistachio brittle

Poached peaches:

1 bottle red wine
1 cup sugar
1 cinnamon stick
1/4 teaspoon nutmeg
2 cloves
1 allspice
Zest of 1 orange
2 peaches halved

Directions:

1| Combine all ingredients except for peaches in a sauce pot and bring to a boil. Stir until sugar is dissolved.

2| Add peaches to poaching liquid. Poach until fork tender.

3| Remove peaches and cool. Slice halved peaches into thirds.

Pistachio Shortbread Cookie Crumbs
Ingredients:
- 3/4 pound softened butter
- 1 cup sugar
- 1 teaspoon vanilla
- 3 1/2 cups all-purpose flour
- 1/4 teaspoon salt
- 1/2 cup crushed pistachio

Directions:
1| Preheat the oven to 350°.

2| In an electric mixer bowl fitted with a paddle attachment, mix together the butter and sugar until they are just combined. Add the vanilla.

3| In a medium bowl, sift together the flour and salt, then add them to the butter-and-sugar mixture. Mix on low speed until the dough starts to form.

4| Dump onto a surface dusted with flour and shape into a flat disk. Wrap in plastic and chill for 30 minutes.

5| Roll the dough 1/2-inch thick and place the cookies on an ungreased baking sheet. Sprinkle with pistachio. Cookie can be left whole because it will be served as dust garnish.

6| Bake for 20-25 minutes, until the edges begin to brown. Allow to cool. Break cookie up by hand or in a food processor.

Red Wine Reduction:
1| Reduce poaching liquid to one cup. Be sure not to not cook too fast or the liquid will become bitter.

2| Reduction will be done when liquid coats the back of a spoon. Add more sugar if the liquid isn't thick enough or if it is bitter.

Orange Mascarpone
Ingredients:
- 1/2 cup mascarpone
- Zest of 1 orange
- 1/4 cup heavy cream
- 2 tablespoons sugar
- Pinch of salt

Directions:
1| Combine all ingredients in a mixer and whip to get air in the mascarpone.

Pistachio brittle
Ingredients:
- Nonstick vegetable oil spray
- 1 cup sugar
- 1/2 cup light corn syrup
- 1 cup unsalted, shelled, raw natural pistachios, coarsely chopped
- 3 tablespoons water
- 1 tablespoon unsalted butter
- 1 teaspoon kosher salt
- 3/4 teaspoon baking soda
- Coarse gray sea salt (such as fleur de sel or sel gris)

Directions:
1| Line a rimmed baking sheet with parchment paper. Spray with nonstick spray and set aside.

2| Whisk sugar, corn syrup, and 3 tablespoons water in a medium saucepan. Stir over medium heat until sugar dissolves. Fit saucepan with candy thermometer, bring mixture to a boil, and cook until thermometer registers 290°, 3-4 minutes.

3| Using a heatproof spatula, stir in pistachios, butter, and kosher salt. Syrup will seize initially, but will melt as it heats back up. Continue to cook syrup, stirring often, until thermometer registers 300° and pistachios are golden brown, 3-4 minutes.

4| Caramel should be pale brown; it will darken slightly as it cools. Sprinkle baking soda over, and stir quickly to blend caramel thoroughly. Mixture will bubble vigorously.

5| Immediately pour caramel onto prepared baking sheet. Using a heatproof spatula, quickly spread out as thin as possible.

6| Sprinkle sea salt over and let caramel cool completely. Break brittle into pieces.

Assembly of Dish:
Micro basil or basil chiffonade

On a round plate make a line of crumbled shortbread from 3 o'clock to 9 o'clock. Place one piece of peach facedown at 9 o'clock, leaning on shortbread. Place one point up in the middle of the plate and one piece of peach at 3 o'clock facedown. Place three dollops of mascarpone on alternating sides of the line of shortbread, in between each peach. Place one piece of cracked brittle on one half of the line of shortbread leaning against one of the peaches. Place another piece on the other end leaning on a peach. Place 1/2 tablespoon of the red wine reduction at 7 o'clock on the plate and drag your spoon through the reduction across to 5 o'clock. Garnish peaches and shortbread with micro basil.

Flourless Chocolate Cake

with Butterscotch Sauce,
Espresso Mousse, Amaro Gelee &
Chocolate Covered Espresso Beans

CHEF RIGATO | YIELD: 1, 12"X17" CAKE

Flourless Chocolate Cake
Ingredients:
- 2 pounds dark chocolate, 60-80% cacao
- 1 1/2 cups butter
- 1 1/3 cup water
- 2 3/4 cups sugar
- 14 eggs

Directions:
1| Chop chocolate and butter. Place in a large bowl.

2| Place water and sugar in a saucepan, and bring to a full boil. Pour liquid over chocolate and butter. Stir until butter is completely melted and mixture is smooth.

3| Whisk eggs, then add to chocolate mixture.

4| Pour into a greased "12x17" sheet tray lined with parchment paper. Place tray onto a larger sheet tray, and put in 350° oven. Pour hot water onto larger sheet tray until half full.

5| Bake 30-40 minutes, until center is firm but jiggles slightly. Place in refrigerator.

Butterscotch Sauce
Ingredients:
- 1/2 cup butter
- 1 2/3 cups brown sugar, packed
- 1/2 cup + 2/3 cup heavy cream
- 1 teaspoon vanilla

Directions:
1| Combine butter, brown sugar and 1/2 cup heavy cream over medium-high heat. Bring to a boil for 5 minutes.

2| Remove from heat and add remaining cream and vanilla. Allow to cool completely.

Espresso Mousse
Ingredients:
- 3 1/2 cups milk
- 1 teaspoon vanilla
- 3/4 cup sugar
- 1/2 teaspoon salt
- 5 teaspoons gelatin
- 2 tablespoons butter
- 1/2 cup espresso
- 1/2 cup milk
- 1/3 cup cornstarch
- 1/3 cup egg yolks
- 2 cups of heavy cream

Directions:
1| Combine first set of ingredients in heavy-bottomed saucepan over medium heat.

2| Whisk together second stage of ingredients (except heavy cream) in a bowl to create a slurry.

3| Bring milk mixture to a boil, and slowly add slurry while whisking constantly. Whisk until mixture thickens and returns to a boil (mixture must come to a boil for cream to thicken properly).

4| Remove from heat, and pour into a pan. Place plastic wrap directly to the surface so no skin forms, and cool completely.

5| Once cream has completely cooled, place into a large bowl, and whisk until smooth. Bring to room temperature.

6| Sprinkle 5 teaspoons of gelatin over 1/2 cup cold water and allow to sit for about 5 minutes.

7| Whip 2 cups of heavy cream to firm peaks, set aside.

8| Melt gelatin until clear and steamy. Working quickly, add gelatin to the espresso cream, whisking until completely combined, and then quickly fold in whipped cream.

Amaro Gelee
Ingredients:
>2 tablespoons gelatin
>1 1/2 cups Amaro Nonino
>1/2 cup water
>1/4 cup sugar

Directions:
1| Bloom gelatin in 1/2 cup cold water.

2| Combine Amaro Nonino, sugar, and water, and heat on stove until sugar is dissolved and mixture is hot. Add gelatin to hot Amaro mixture.

3| Pour into a tray that has been lined with plastic wrap. Allow to cool and set completely. Cut into desired shape/size.

Chocolate Covered Espresso Beans
Ingredients:
>8 ounces chocolate
>1 cup espresso beans

Directions:
1| Melt chocolate and pour over espresso beans. Stir, then pour onto parchment paper.

2| Allow chocolate to set completely, and finely chop.

Assembly of Dish:
Flip cake out of pan, and remove parchment paper. Flip back over, and using a knife that's been dipped in hot water, portion into desired size. Place butterscotch on plate, then cake, and pipe espresso mousse onto plate. Garnish with espresso beans and Amaro gelee.

■

Pistachio Financier
Meyer Lemon Curd, Honey Crème Fraîche, Caramelized Sugar & Lavender

CHEF RIGATO | SERVES: 4-6

Pistachio Financier
Ingredients:
>1 pound butter
>3 cups pistachios, ground
>3 1/2 cups powdered sugar
>1 cup + 2 tablespoons all-purpose flour
>1/2 teaspoons salt
>1 1/2 cups egg whites

Directions:
1| Dice butter, and place in saucepan over medium heat. Cook, stirring often, until a nut-brown color is achieved. Set aside.

2| Combine ground pistachios, powdered sugar, flour, and salt.

3| Whisk egg whites until frothy, and add to dry ingredients, mixing until blended. Add brown butter, and mix well.

4| Pour into a greased "12x17" sheet tray that has been lined with parchment paper.

5| Bake at 350° until golden, about 15-20 minutes.

Meyer Lemon Curd
Ingredients:

- 1 tablespoon + 1 teaspoon powdered gelatin
- 2 cups Meyer lemon juice
- 4 cups sugar
- 6 eggs
- 1/2 cup egg yolks
- 8 ounces butter
- 2 lemons, zested

Directions:

1| Sprinkle gelatin over 1/2 cup cold water, and set aside.

2| Combine lemon juice, sugar, and egg yolks in a thick-bottomed saucepan. Over medium heat, cook mixture, stirring constantly, until thickened and reaches 180°.

3| Remove from heat, and strain. While mixture is still hot, add gelatin, butter, and lemon zest.

4| Once all of the butter and gelatin has melted, pour over cooled pistachio financier, and place in freezer.

Caramelized Sugar Garnish
Ingredients:

- Granulated sugar

Directions:

1| Sprinkle an even layer of granulated sugar onto a silicone baking mat. Bake at 350°, until sugar has completely melted and turned golden brown.

2| Once cool, break into pieces and use as garnish.

Honey Crème Fraîche
Ingredients:

- Honey, to taste
- 1 cup crème fraîche

Directions:

1| Add honey to crème fraîche until desired taste is achieved.

Assembly of Dish:

Once lemon curd has frozen completely, cut along edges of sheet tray, flip curd and cake out of the pan, and remove parchment paper. Flip back onto a cutting board. Portion into desired shape and size.

Place crème fraiche onto a plate. Put the curd on top, then garnish with caramelized sugar, and a few dried lavender flowers.

■

Variations of Chocolate & Beet
with Fall Raspberries & Black Pepper Ice Cream

CHEF JOHNS | SERVES: 4-6

Bittersweet Chocolate Crémeux
Ingredients:

- 6 tablespoons sugar
- 60 grams egg yolk
- 1/2 cup cream
- 1 cup milk
- 1 1/2 cups bittersweet chocolate, chopped finely
- 1 teaspoon salt, or to taste

Directions:

1| In a bowl, whisk yolks and half the sugar until smooth.

2| Put cream, milk, and the rest of the sugar into a small saucepan over medium heat. Bring to a hard simmer.

3| Pour some of the hot milk mixture into the yolk mixture and whisk until smooth.

4| Pour tempered egg mixture back into heated milk mixture and put on low heat. Stir constantly with a spatula until it thickens enough to coat the back of a metal spoon.

5| Remove from heat and pour into a clean bowl.

6| Add the chocolate. Let it sit for a minute to allow the chocolate to melt.

7| Whisk until mixture is smooth. Season with salt.

8| Cover the creamy surface directly with plastic wrap. Refrigerate for at least 2 hours.

Black Pepper Ice Cream
Ingredients:
120 grams egg yolk
3/4 cup sugar
2 cups cream
1 cup milk
1 tablespoon freshly ground black pepper
Salt, to taste

Directions:
1| Whisk egg yolks and half the sugar in a bowl.

2| Put cream, milk, the rest of the sugar, and black pepper in a pot over medium heat. Bring almost to a boil.

3| Temper the hot liquid into the egg yolk mixture.

4| Whisk all back into the pot over low heat. Mix until the mixture coats the back of a metal spoon.

5| Strain into a container over an ice bath, and cool overnight.

6| Season with salt and run in an ice cream machine.

Raspberry-Beet Purée
Ingredients:
2 large red beets
12 ounces raspberries
1/2 cup sugar
1 tablespoon lemon juice
Salt, to taste

Directions:
1| Boil beets in salted water until tender. Cool in ice bath. Peel skin. Purée in a food processor until fine. Cool.

2| In a Vitamix, blend raspberries with half the beet purée on high until smooth.

3| Mix in sugar and lemon juice. Season with salt.

Chocolate Crumbs
Ingredients:
90 grams butter, room temperature
90 grams flour
85 grams sugar
30 grams 100% cocoa
1 gram salt

Directions:
1| In a standing mixer, using the paddle attachment, mix all ingredients until it forms one smooth mass.

2| Break apart into pieces on a parchment-lined, half sheet tray.

3| Preheat oven to 375°. Cook for 7-10 minutes. Mix around on sheet tray and rotate.

4| Cook for another 5-7 minutes until dark. Cool for 30 minutes.

5| Pulse 10-15 times in a food processor until fine crumbs form.

Chocolate Tuiles
Ingredients:
3/4 cup + 2 1/2 tablespoons flour
1/4 cup honey
1/4 pound butter
1 cup powdered sugar
1 1/2 tablespoons cocoa
1/4 cup egg whites
Stencil of your choice

Directions:

1| Sift dry ingredients together.

2| In a stand mixer, using the paddle attachment, cream honey and butter until smooth.

3| Add sifted dry ingredients and egg whites.

4| Mix on high for 5 minutes until smooth. Stop and scrape down sides of bowl a couple of times. Chill tuile batter overnight.

5| Preheat oven to 300°.

6| Using a small palette knife, spread batter evenly over stencil onto silpat-lined sheet tray. Lift stencil. Repeat until sheet tray is filled.

7| Bake until dry. This depends on stencil size. For a 2-inch circle stencil, it takes about 10 minutes.

8| Dry for 5 minutes. Immediately store in an air-tight container.

Candied Beet

Ingredients:

1 cup sugar

1 cup water

1 large beet, sliced paper thin on mandoline

Directions:

1| Make 50 percent simple syrup by combining 1 cup water and 1 cup sugar. Bring to a simmer until all sugar dissolves.

2| Add sliced beets. Simmer for 1-2 minutes until almost translucent. Take off heat and cool/store in the syrup. Strain beets when ready to use.

Assembly of Dish:

Scatter fresh raspberries on plate. Put crémeux in a piping bag with a 1/2-inch tip. Pipe small mounds of crémeux between raspberries. Put purée in a squeeze bottle. Squeeze purée between raspberries. Spoon a small mound of chocolate crumbs on edge of raspberries. Top crumbs with a quenelle of black pepper ice cream. Garnish with bull's blood microgreens, candied beets, and broken pieces of chocolate tuile.

Frozen Amaretto Sabayon

with Citrus Mint Salad & Pine Nut Granola

CHEF GREEN | SERVES: 6

Ingredients:

6 egg yolks

1 1/4 cup fresh cream

1/2 cup amaretto liquor

Directions:

1| Whisk egg yolks with cream in large metal mixing bowl until smooth, then add amaretto liquor and continue mixing.

2| Boil 1/4 cup water in a saucepan then turn to low heat. Place bowl on saucepan rim and whisk for 10 minutes. Whisk constantly so the mixture does not cook.

3| Pour mixture into another bowl and keep stirring for 5 minutes until cool.

4| Pour into a metal container and place into freezer.

5| Allow to freeze for several hours before using.

Chef Ward

JOE MUER SEAFOOD

Chef Eric Ward has served as executive chef for Joe Muer Seafood in Detroit since 2012. Under Ward's direction, Joe Muer Seafood was selected as *Hour Detroit's* 2012 Restaurant of the Year. Previously, Ward held the corporate chef position at Matt Prentice Restaurant Group, executive chef at Coach Insignia, Novi Chophouse, Northern Lakes Seafood Co., Shiraz, and vice president of Culinary Endeavors Winter Park, Colo.

Chef Yagihashi

SLURPING TURTLE

Takashi Yagihashi opened his namesake Chicago restaurant, Takashi, in December 2007 to immediate critical and consumer success, receiving a Michelin star for five consecutive years. Takashi might've closed at the end of 2014, but Yagihashi remains in the kitchen. Both *Esquire* and *Chicago* magazines named Takashi "Best New Restaurant" in 2008, and Yagihashi garnered a rating of 29 in Zagat, the highest food rating in Chicago. Yagihashi also operates Noodles by Takashi Yagihashi, a rustic Japanese noodle restaurant that opened in 2006 at Macy's on State Street in Chicago. Yagihashi has also run famed kitchens like Okada at the Wynn Hotel in Las Vegas, and Tribute in Detroit.

In 2000, Yagihashi graced the cover of *Food and Wine* as one of America's 10 "Best New Chefs", and in 2003, he was selected "Best Chef: Midwest" by the esteemed James Beard Foundation. His first cookbook, *Takashi's Noodles*, was released in April 2009.

In 2011, Slurping Turtle brought Japanese comfort food to Chicago's River North neighborhood, becoming an instant success and earning a Michelin Bib Gourmand Award in 2013. And in 2014, Slurping Turtle expanded to Ann Arbor where the delicate balance and respect for natural flavors continues to be a hallmark of his cooking style. Yagihashi has competed on *Top Chef Masters*, where he was awarded "fan favorite", *Iron Chef*, and appeared on the *Martha Stewart Show*, and *Top Chef* as a judge. In 2014, Yagihashi also competed against former *Top Chef* and *Top Chef Masters* personalities in a new Bravo series, *Top Chef Duels*.

Japanese Green Tea Soufflé

with Honey Ginger Crème Anglaise & Black Sesame Cookie

CHEF CONSTANTINE | SERVES: 6-8

Ingredients:

1/4 pound butter
1/4 pound flour
2 cups milk
2 teaspoon ground ginger powder
1 teaspoon vanilla extract
4 1/2 ounces egg yolks
6 ounces egg whites
6 ounces sugar
2 tablespoons Japanese green tea powder

For Coating Ramekins:

1/2 tablespoon unsalted butter
at room temperature
4 teaspoons granulated sugar

Directions:

1| Preheat oven to 400°. Prepare the soufflé cups by buttering and coating them with sugar.

2| Melt butter in a medium saucepan. When melted whisk in flour and cook for 1 minute. Add milk and ginger. Cook until the mixture looks like it's pulling away from the sides.

3| Remove from heat and place mixture in a stand mixer bowl with a paddle and beat until mixture is cool. When mixture is cooled add the egg yolks and vanilla extract. Mix until combined.

4| Place mixture in a large moon bowl. Place egg whites in clean mixing bowl with whisk attachment on medium power. Combine sugar and green tea powder, and rain sugar mixture into the egg whites. Whisk to stiff peaks.

5| Fold the whites into the base and portion into the soufflé cups. Place on baking sheet and bake for 15-20 minutes or until light brown. Remove and serve immediately.

Spicy Black Sesame Cookies

Ingredients:

- 1 stick unsalted butter
- 5 3/5 ounces all-purpose flour
- 1 2/5 ounces almond meal
- 2 4/5 ounces sugar
- Salt, to taste
- 1 2/5 ounces black sesame seeds
- 1 egg yolk
- 1/4 teaspoon ground cayenne pepper

Directions:

1| Cut the butter into small cubes and keep them refrigerated until ready to use.

2| In food processor, combine the flour, almond meal, sugar, salt, cayenne, and half the sesame seeds. Blend the flour, sesame seed mixture for 1 minute.

3| Add the cold diced butter and blend for 30 seconds or until the mixture looks like coarse meal.

4| Add egg yolk and remaining sesame seeds. Blend until combined. Remove from food processor bowl and mix ingredients if not well combined.

5| Form the dough into a ball and cut in half. Roll it into a log approximately 2 inches across. The rolling process is easier if the dough is wrapped in plastic wrap.

6| Refrigerate until firm, about 1 hour.

7| Preheat oven to 350°. Remove the dough from the plastic wrap and cut into discs about 1/4-inch thick.

8| Place the cookies on two baking sheets lined with parchment paper. Bake for 12-15 minutes or until lightly browned around the edges.

9| Remove from oven and allow to cool on the baking sheet for about 10 minutes. Then transfer to a wire rack to cool completely.

Honey Ginger Crème Anglaise

Ingredients:

- 2 cups heavy cream
- 1 cup milk
- 1/2 vanilla bean, split and scraped
- 1/4 cup honey
- 2 tablespoons ginger, minced
- 6 large egg yolks
- 1/4 cup granulated sugar
- 1 tablespoon powdered sugar

Directions:

1| Heat the heavy cream, milk, vanilla bean, honey, and minced ginger in a large saucepan over medium heat.

2| Place the egg yolks and sugar in a heatproof mixing bowl and beat until pale yellow in color and all of the sugar has dissolved. Temper about 1/2 cup of the cream mixture into the egg mixture and whisk vigorously to incorporate well.

3| Add the egg mixture to the saucepan with the cream mixture and cook, stirring constantly with a whisk or wooden spoon. Be sure to stir in the corners of the pot and lower the heat slightly.

4| Stir the mixture for 4-5 minutes, or until the custard has thickened enough to coat the back of a spoon. Remove from the stove and strain the custard through a fine mesh sieve into a clean bowl.

5| Place the bowl in another bowl half-filled with ice and water to cool the custard. To chill the custard faster, stir it occasionally with a spoon.

Mousse al Cioccolato

Valrhona Dark Chocolate, Chocolate Espresso, Tuile, Caramel, Cashews & Vanilla Gelato

CHEF DEL SIGNORE | SERVES: 6

Chocolate Espresso Tuile

Ingredients:

200 grams all-purpose flour

30 grams cocoa

225 grams sugar

225 grams egg whites

170 grams melted butter (room temp.)

30 grams ground espresso

Directions:

1| Mix together flour, cocoa, and sugar. Whisk in egg whites, butter, and ground espresso until smooth.

2| Spread batter onto silpat mat in 4-inch by 1/2-inch rectangles. Bake at 350° until cooked.

3| Immediately pull the tuiles from the silpat, and wrap into a ring shape. They will harden as they cool.

Dark Chocolate Mousse

Ingredients:

660 grams cream

135 grams eggs

150 grams egg yolks

210 grams sugar

465 grams Valrhona chocolate (66%)

Directions:

1| Whip cream to soft peaks. Prepare eggs and yolk in a mixer with a whip attachment.

2| Cook sugar on the stove to 240°.

3| Turn mixer with eggs to low speed, and slowly pour in the cooked sugar along the side of the bowl. Once the sugar is incorporated turn the speed to high, and whip eggs until they are thick, pale, and ribbony. Meanwhile, melt chocolate over a double boiler.

4| Once eggs and chocolate are ready, pour half of the chocolate into the eggs, and whisk rapidly. Once chocolate is about half mixed in, add the remaining chocolate, and mix until mostly incorporated.

5| Add half the whipped cream and fold it gently into the mixture. Once cream is halfway mixed in, add the rest, and fold until incorporated.

Vanilla Caramel

Ingredients:

550 grams sugar

425 grams glucose syrup

1 vanilla bean

725 grams cream

85 grams butter

Directions:

1| Cook sugar, glucose, and vanilla to a dark amber color. Pour in cream and let the caramel come back to a boil. Turn down heat and gently simmer until cream has reduced.

2| Incorporate butter and chill.

Chocolate Square:

120 grams fondant

80 grams glucose

80 grams dark chocolate

Directions:

1| Cook glucose and fondant to 310°, and pour over dark chocolate. Mix to incorporate.

2| Roll out as thin as possible onto a silpat mat. Break the sugar into small pieces and reheat in the oven. As soon as the sugar is cool enough to peel off the mat, take it and stretch it out gently to form into your desired shape.

Candied Cashews

> **600 grams cashews**
> **240 grams sugar**
> **Water**
> **30 grams butter**

Directions:

1| Roast cashews lightly. Cook sugar and water on stove to 240°. Add in the roasted nuts, and stir constantly until sugar is golden brown. Add butter and incorporate. Spread nuts out on a tray to cool.

Assembly of Dish:

> **Chocolate Espresso Tuile**
> **Vanilla Gelato**
> **Espresso Macaroon**

Place chocolate espresso tuile in the center of the plate, and pipe chocolate mousse to fill the inside. Top with a tempered chocolate square. Spoon caramel sauce over the top of the square, ensuring it falls over the sides equally. Wedge the chocolate sugar tuile in between a scoop of vanilla gelato, and an espresso macaroon. Sprinkle candied nuts over the top.

Roasted White Chocolate Panna Cotta

with Blackberry Compote

CHEF SOMERVILLE | SERVES: 2

Blackberry Compote
Ingredients:

> **2 cups blackberry purée**
> **1 cups sugar**
> **6 sheets gelatin, bloomed**
> **1/4 cup glucose**

Directions:

1| Bring purée and sugar to a light boil.

2| Remove from heat. Add the gelatin sheets, and glucose.

White Chocolate Panna Cotta
Ingredients:

> **225 grams cream cheese, softened**
> **115 grams sugar**
> **1 vanilla bean, scraped**
> **340 grams heavy cream**
> **3 gelatin sheets, bloomed**
> **225 grams roasted white chocolate**
> **Acetate sheets**
> **Blackberry compte**
> **Fresh mixed berries, to finish**

Directions:

1| Beat cream cheese, sugar, and vanilla.

2| Scald 120 grams cream. Add gelatin. When dissolved add chocolate.

3| Whip remaining 220 grams of cream to soft peaks. Fold into chocolate mixture. Cool.

4| Line 2 1/2-inch vertical molds with acetate. Pipe mixture into mold. Top neatly with blackberry compote. Freeze overnight.

5| When ready to plate bring molds to room temperature. Unmold. Decorate with assorted berries.

1

2

1| Chocolate vs. Cheese. *Chef Rigato.*

2| Red Wine Poached Peach with
Whipped Mascarpone and Pistachio
Shortbread Cookie. *Chef Polisei.*

Cocktails

The Sugar House bar was opened in Detroit in 2011 by Dave Kwiatkowski because at the time there wasn't a craft cocktail bar in the city. Drinking at this bar is a one-of-a-kind experience where the bartenders treat their craft as an art form and create each drink meticulously. Next time you're in Corktown, stop in. But for now, try whipping up one of their cocktails at home.

Sugar House Manhattan

Ingredients:
1 1/2 ounces Maker's 46 Bourbon
1/2 ounce Cynar
3/4 ounce sweet vermouth
Bitters, to taste
Cucumber slice

Directions:
Stir all ingredients except cucumber in a rocks glass, and serve neat or on ice. Add a cucumber slice to garnish.

Cucumber Spritz

Ingredients:
1 1/2 ounces Effen Cucumber Vodka
1/2 ounce lemon juice
1/2 ounce simple syrup
Cava, to taste
Cucumber slice

Directions:
Combine first three ingredients into a shaker, and shake. Strain over a coupe glass, top with cava, and add a cucumber slice for garnish.

Vodka Basil Smash

Ingredients:

2 ounces Tito's Handmade Vodka
1/2 ounce lemon
1/2 ounce simple syrup
4-6 basil leaves

Directions:

Combine ingredients in a shaker. Shake, and double strain on the rocks. Add a basil leaf for garnish.

Pama Spritz

Ingredients:

1/4 ounce lemon juice
4 ounces cava
1 ounce Pama pomegranate liqueur

Directions:

Add ingredients to a coupe glass: First the lemon, then cava, then Pama.

Bourbon Manhattan

Ingredients:

1 1/2 ounces Elijah Craig 12-year Bourbon
3/4 ounce Punt e Mes
2 dashes Angostura bitters
Orange peel

Directions:

Stir in a shaker, and strain over a rocks glass. Serve neat with an orange peel twist.

Skeleton Key

Ingredients:

2 ounces Elijah Craig 12-year Bourbon
1/2 ounce elderflower liqueur
1/2 ounce lemon juice
1/2 ounce ginger syrup
Angostura, to taste
Splash of soda

Directions:

Combine first four ingredients in a shaker, and shake. Strain over a tall Collins glass, top with Angostura, and add a splash of soda.

El Diablo: Hornitos

Ingredients:

2 ounces Plata Tequila
1/2 ounce ginger syrup
1/2 ounce lime juice
Soda, to taste
1/4 ounce crème de cassis

Directions:

Combine ingredients into a shaker (minus cassis), and shake. Add cassis to the bottom of a tall glass and strain the shaker contents over an ice-filled glass. Top with soda.

Vodka Caipirinha

Ingredients:

> 2 ounces Tito's Handmade Vodka
> 1/2 muddled lime
> 1 ounce simple syrup

Directions:

Combine ingredients in a rocks glass, and stir with crushed ice.

Pama Daisy

Ingredients:

> 1 1/2 ounces Tito's Handmade Vodka
> 3/4 ounce Pama pomegranate liqueur
> 1/2 ounce lemon juice
> 1/4 ounce simple syrup

Directions:

Combine ingredients in a shaker, and shake. Strain over a coupe glass.

Texas 75

Ingredients:

> 1 1/2 ounces Tito's Handmade Vodka
> 1/2 ounce lemon juice
> 1/2 ounce simple syrup
> Cava, to taste
> Lemon peel

Directions:

Combine first three ingredients in a shaker, and shake. Strain over a coupe glass, top with cava, and garnish with lemon peel twist.

Cucumber Crush

Ingredients:

> 2 ounces Effen Cucumber Vodka
> 1/4 ounce lemon juice
> 1/2 ounce grapefruit juice
> 1/2 ounce hibiscus syrup
> Soda, to finish
> Mint leaves

Directions:

Combine liquid ingredients into a shaker, and shake over a tall glass. Top with soda, and garnish with mint leaves

El Conquistador

Ingredients:

> 1 1/2 ounces Hornitos Plata Tequila
> 3/4 ounces Pedro Ximenez
> 1/2 ounce lemon juice
> Grated cinnamon

Directions:

Combine liquid ingredients into a shaker, and shake. Strain over a coupe glass, and add grated cinnamon to garnish.

Molecular Mule

Ingredients:

> 2 ounces Tito's Handmade Vodka
> 1/2 ounce lemon juice
> 1/2 ounce ginger syrup
> Mint foam

Directions:

Combine ingredients in a shaker, and shake. Strain, and serve neat over a small rocks glass. Top with mint foam.

Kentucky Mule

Ingredients:

> 2 ounces Maker's 46 Bourbon
> 1/2 ounce lime juice
> 1/2 ounce ginger syrup
> Soda, to taste
> Mint leaf

Directions:

Combine first three ingredients in a shaker, and shake. Strain over a tall Collins glass, top with soda, and add a mint leaf garnish.

Tiger in the Jungle

Ingredients:

> 2 ounces Cruzan Rum
> 1/4 ounce cinnamon simple syrup
> Bitters, to taste
> Grapefruit peel

Directions:

Combine ingredients in a rocks glass, and stir. Garnish with a grapefruit peel.

St. Croix Daiquiri

Ingredients:

> 2 ounces Cruzan Rum
> 1/2 ounce lime juice
> 1/2 ounce pomegranate syrup
> Bitters, to taste

Directions:

Combine ingredients in a shaker, and shake. Strain if desired over a rocks glass.

Pama Swizzle

Ingredients:

> 1 1/2 ounces Tito's Handmade Vodka
> 3/4 ounce Pama pomegranate liqueur
> 3/4 ounce lime
> Mint leaves
> 1/4 ounce simple syrup

Directions:

Combine first three ingredients in a tall/highball glass. Muddle the mint. Swizzle stir the drink with crushed ice.

INDEX Page numbers in **boldface** indicate photographs.

AGNOLOTTI: A type of pasta typical of the Piedmont region of Italy. Pasta squares stuffed with a variety of fillings, similar to ravioli.

BLOOMING GELATIN:
As the gelatin absorbs the liquid, each granule becomes enlarged; this is known as "blooming." Blooming gelatin is a step integral to ensuring the smooth texture of a finished product. It involves sprinkling the powdered gelatin into a liquid and letting it sit for 3 to 5 minutes. Then, when the mixture is heated, the gelatin will dissolve evenly.

1| Sprinkle or "rain" the powdered gelatin evenly over its softening liquid to keep lumps from forming.

2| Set the gelatin aside for a few minutes until it swells or "blooms" as it absorbs the liquid.

3| Melt the gelatin either in a hot water bath or in a microwave (for about 10 seconds on high) until it becomes translucent. Use your fingers to check that all the granules have totally dissolved.

BRUNOISE: A precision cut where the food is first julienned (cut into thin matchsticks), then turned a quarter turn and diced again thus producing tiny cubes with equal sides (under 3 mm). This cut is commonly used as a garnish for consommé, or fine salsas.

CHINOIS: A cone-shaped sieve with a closely woven mesh for straining sauces.

RILLETTE: A preparation of meat similar to pâté. Commonly made from pork, the meat is cubed or chopped, salted heavily and cooked slowly in fat until it is tender enough to be easily shredded, and then cooled with enough of the fat to form a paste.

SLURRY: A combination of starch (usually cornstarch, flour, potato starch or arrowroot) and cold water, which is mixed together and used to thicken a soup or sauce. If the starch is solely added directly to a hot liquid, the starch granules cannot disperse easily and clumps form. Once mixed with water, the slurry can be added directly to the hot liquid. The liquid must be brought up to a simmer each time to ensure the starch reaches its full thickening potential before more is added. Add a bit at a time until you reach the desired consistency.

JULIENNE: A culinary knife cut in which the food item is cut into long thin strips, similar to matchsticks. Sometimes called shoe "string".

QUENELLE:
- In French cooking, an oval-shaped dumpling of finely chopped fish or meat that is poached in water or stock and usually served with a sauce.
- In desserts, typically a football shaped scoop of ice cream or mousse. With a spoon in each hand, scoop a generous amount of mousse into one spoon. Gently press the bowl of the second spoon against the mousse, scooping the contents from the first spoon into the second. Transfer the mousse back to the first spoon in the same manner. This begins to create a smooth, rounded surface where the mousse is molded to the spoon. Keep scooping back and forth until you have a nice, smooth oval shape.

QUENELLE TEST: A test to check for seasoning: wrap a heaping tablespoon in plastic wrap and poach it in water for about 10 minutes. Taste the quenelle and adjust seasoning if necessary.

PIPE: To squeeze a pastry bag in order to force frosting or other paste-like mixtures through the tip of the bag for the purpose of decorating or creating special shapes.

METRIC CONVERSION FORMULAS

TO CONVERT:	DO THIS:
• Centimeters to inches	divide centimeters by 2.54
• Cups to liters	multiply cups by 0.236
• Cups to milliliters	multiply cups by 236.59
• Gallons to liters	multiply gallons by 3.785
• Grams to ounces	divide grams by 28.35
• Inches to centimeters	multiply inches by 2.54
• Kilograms to pounds	divide kilograms by 0.454
• Liters to cups	divide liters by 0.236
• Liters to gallons	divide liters by 3.785
• Liters to pints	divide liters by 0.473
• Liters to quarts	divide liters by 0.946
• Milliliters to cups	divide milliliters by 236.59
• Milliliters to fluid ounces	divide milliliters by 29.57
• Milliliters to tablespoons	divide milliliters by 14.79
• Milliliters to teaspoons	divide milliliters by 4.93
• Ounces to grams	multiply ounces by 28.35
• Ounces to milliliters	multiply ounces by 29.57
• Pints to liters	multiply pints by 0.473
• Pounds to kilograms	multiply pounds by 0.454
• Quarts to liters	multiply quarts by 0.946
• Tablespoons to milliliters	multiply tablespoons by 14.79
• Teaspoons to milliliters	multiply teaspoons by 4.93

HOUR
DETROIT

SAVOR DETROIT SPONSORS

Winebow

pixelprint.us

GLEANERS FOOD BANK
of Southeastern Michigan

Veritas Distributors, Inc.
AMERICAN & IMPORTED WINES

PAMA
POMEGRANATE LIQUEUR

★ NWS ★
Michigan, Inc.